The

OUTDOOR
Survival
manual

The
OUTDOOR
Survival
manual

First published in 2001 by New Holland (Publishers) Ltd

London • Cape Town • Sydney • Auckland

86 Edgware Road
London, W2 2EA
United Kingdom

80 McKenzie Street,
Cape Town 8001,
South Africa

14 Aquatic Drive,
Frenchs Forest,
NSW 2086,
Australia

218 Lake Road,
Northcote,
Auckland,
New Zealand

ISBN 1 85974 712 4 (hardback)
ISBN 1 85974 713 2 (paperback)

Publisher: *Mariëlle Renssen*
Managing Editors: *Claudia Dos Santos, Mari Roberts*
Managing Art Editor: *Peter Bosman*
Editor: *Lauren Copley*
Designer: *Lyndall du Toit*
Illustrators: *Steven Felmore and Chip Snaddon*
Proofreader: *Sean Fraser*
Picture Researcher: *Sonya Meyer*
Production: *Myrna Collins*
Medical consultant and co-author (sections/chapters as listed above): *Dr Lance Michell*
Consultant (UK): *Mick Tyler*

Reproduction by Unifoto (Pty) Ltd
Printed and bound in Malaysia by Times Offset (M) Sdn. Bhd.

PAGE 1: The Utah desert, with a well-lit tent providing security and shelter.

PAGES 2 & 3: Wide open expanses like this terrain in the Yosemite mountains are what attract hikers.

RIGHT: Footsteps in the sand are all that humans should aim to leave behind when visiting wilderness areas.

PAGE 6: Scenery blurs together in dense forests, making accurate navigation vital.

PAGE 7 TOP TO BOTTOM: A carefully managed fire is a great morale booster and also provides heat; some useful tools for catching fish, a good source of food; a warm meal and shelter are two prime requirements; a rope and knotmaking skills can be vital; experience in map-reading and navigation is integral to survival.

CHAPTER OPENERS

CHAPTER 1: High-altitude travel requires specialist knowledge and preparation.

CHAPTER 2: The further one ventures into true wilderness, the greater the need for appropriate kit.

CHAPTER 3: When faced with a survival situation, focus on your priorities — shelter, food, clothing and water.

CHAPTER 4: Moving as a close-knit group is vital, particularly in heavily wooded areas.

CHAPTER 5: Without professional medical help, some survivors have to use common sense and first aid principles.

CHAPTER 6: Smoke flares prove useful wind- and location indicators for rescuers.

CHAPTER 7: Natural phenomena such as this 'twister' can lead to dire situations.

AUTHOR'S ACKNOWLEDGEMENTS

First and foremost, thanks to the design and editorial team at New Holland Publishers, Cape Town, ever professional but still full of life and laughter, for keeping their cool in the face of mountains of material and eventually organizing it into a cohesive whole.

To the editor Lauren Copley, who kept the sense of things while chipping away at excess verbiage and designer Lyndall du Toit who arranged text and pictures into an aesthetic masterpiece. Thanks also to Simon Pooley who tactfully but firmly kept things on track.

A special word of appreciation must also go to the Outdoor Warehouse chain of stores, for the use and loan of top-class outdoor gear; also to Duncan and Orca Industries, Manex Marine and Karrimor for loans of gear for photographic shoots.

To Jacques – thank you for your patience and photographic expertise; to the photographic models – particularly Johan, Tessa, Zirc, Willem, Peter, Frans, Heino and John; as well as Cara and Kerrin – your enthusiasm and hours of help are greatly appreciated.

Lastly to Dr Lance Michell, for advice on the manuscript as a whole, as well as for taking on the task of writing an up-to-date and expert medical section – thank you for your invaluable input.

CONTENTS

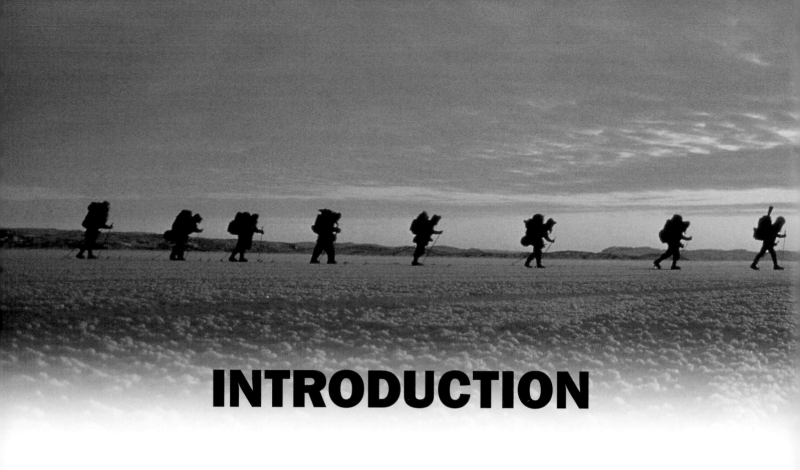

INTRODUCTION

'Survival' has recently become a buzz word, with popular television programmes portraying dramatic episodes of groups being challenged to perform in 'survival situations'. Some of the scenarios indeed give a glimpse of what true survival would entail in real life. They all share one great dissimilarity from an actual survival incident – all the survival participants in these television programmes know that rescue and civilization are close to hand. In a real survival predicament, however, people are suddenly thrust into a stressful and unfamiliar situation. Often, they are uncertain when and how they will be rescued and in many cases, they are inadequately prepared to handle the rigours of having to cope and survive in the outdoors, both in terms of practical knowledge and appropriate equipment.

Uncertainty remains one of the major stresses of survival. The concept of survival – confronting and overcoming a set of challenges – is something most people experience and can handle every day when they are in their familiar life territory. Each outdoor survival situation is unique; there are no guaranteed formulas to ensure that individuals are able to handle the challenges.

TOP An expedition prepares to challenge the extreme conditions on Baffin Island, Canada.
ABOVE Using pre-learnt skills makes it easier to build a rough sleeping platform.

The growing popularity in hiking, adventure travel and various outdoor sporting activities such as canoeing, mountain biking and camping has seen an exponential increase in the number of accidents in wilderness areas. Perhaps of even more concern is that many serious survival situations arise out of ordinary family walks or treks into innocuous-looking wilderness areas by groups and adventure travel enthusiasts.

Whether you need to survive because of natural phenomena, accidents, bad planning or simply bad luck, the aim of *The Outdoor Survival Manual* is to demystify survival in unfamiliar territory and conditions. This is done by providing practical, down-to-earth advice on the most common problem areas of survival. For convenience, the manual is divided into colour-coded chapters, each dealing with a particular key theme. These are survival principles, equipment, first priorities, movement,

medical know-how, communication and interaction, as well as extreme survival skills. For the family, outdoor enthusiast or youth group, the manual outlines a host of useful skills and guidelines that will make ordinary adventure trips more enjoyable, especially if practised in advance. For the dedicated wilderness traveller, it aims to offer invaluable survival-related information that could be life-saving.

Planning is the key

Whether you are going on a short camping trip with family members, are part of an organized hiking group or simply an outdoor enthusiast who enjoys experiencing nature, thorough advance planning is a vital element for anyone venturing into the outdoors. Problems occur in many cases because groups do not plan their trips and their preparation is inadequate. The manual offers sound advice on appropriate kit for different environments to ensure that you have all the

essentials to handle whatever comes your way. Equally important is knowledge of the wilderness area you are heading for, and learning any adventure activities you intend doing such as canoeing, climbing or river rafting. Physical preparedness and ensuring you have an appropriate level of physical fitness are other essential prerequisites to a safe and enjoyable outdoor adventure.

Focus on practical skills

Practical outdoor and survival skills including map-reading, navigation, knots and lashing, creating shelters and bridges, river crossing techniques, finding food and water, making fires and improvisation receive considerable attention in this manual. Many of the techniques are not for normal everyday use and should only be applied in genuine survival situations. They should, however, be practised in advance. This would enhance outdoor experiences

and improve your coping skills in a real-life emergency. Consider yourself fortunate if you never need to use the information in this manual. However, if just some advice is able to benefit and be useful to an outdoor traveller in a survival predicament, then it will have achieved its primary goal.

A mosquito net is an essential, not a luxury item in regions that are known to have a high malaria risk.

SURVIVAL PRINCIPLES

SURVIVAL PRINCIPLES

The very nature of survival situations is that they often arise when one least expects them. Few people knowingly place themselves in minimalized positions where their very existence is at stake. However, the growth in adventure sports such as off-piste skiing, kayaking, climbing, mountaineering, back-country hiking, micro-light flying and sailing has meant that more people are suddenly finding themselves in life-and-death situations. A large number of recent survival incidents have involved backpackers, 4x4 enthusiasts, snowmobiles or small boats. It is fair to say that most survival situations have been unanticipated by the persons concerned, although this is not to say that they arose inevitably – human fallibility often has a good deal to do with it.

A very useful guideline is to always play the prophet of doom and bank on a 'worst case' scenario when taking a trip into the great outdoors. Cater for the worst in anticipated weather and for the longest expected time, then add extra to both. If an emergency does arise, you'll be better prepared in terms of essentials such as clothing, shelter, food and medical supplies.

Avoiding survival situations

Perhaps the most self-evident thing is to try to avoid getting into survival situations in the first place. There are unfortunate times when one can do absolutely nothing to prevent this – a commercial aeroplane crash, the wreck of a pleasure liner and entirely

ABOVE Before setting out on any hike, ensure that you are equipped with vital skills such as navigation and route finding.

unpredictable natural disasters such as earthquakes, tornadoes, hurricanes or freak avalanches. However, many incidents arise because an individual

or group is inadequately prepared for the area or the activity and is thus unable to cope with the conditions. An important consideration should always be 'Have I the right equipment for the task, and enough of it?' Equally important is to ask 'Do I have sufficient background and knowledge for the task?'

There is often no substitute for experience – this adage is frequently forgotten in the information overload of our modern, fast-paced world. Going deep into back-country woods on an adventure trip in the middle of winter is hardly a suitable activity for novice hikers – yet a surprising number of rookie groups do just this, often with sadly predictable and even fatal consequences.

This is not to say 'Stay at home, and never go hiking or exploring the outdoors.' Far from it – outdoors and adventure activities provide a magnificent escape from the stresses of everyday life, and can have great character-building benefits. What is important, however, is to match the activity or the level of the activity to your experience and that of the group. To take a group of amateur climbers on an extreme climbing expedition in the Canadian Rockies would be courting disaster, no matter how experienced the leader may be. It may just be the leader who dies or is injured during the trip.

The focus of this manual is to help outdoor adventurers be better equipped when things go radically wrong and survival is at stake.

If you are a parent reading this, make sure that your entire family is informed – they might end up being the ones who need the knowledge, or the only ones capable of using it. And if you are one of the younger members of your family, persuade your parents and older siblings to read this book.

It would certainly do no harm to study and practise some of the principles covered on these pages, and it might make the difference between life and death. At the very least, it may enhance your experience of a recreational outdoor experience.

TOP Thorough research is the basis for a successful and well-organized adventure experience. Fail to prepare and you may run the risk of unpleasant or downright serious situations. Guide books are not the only useful 'tools', however. Through powerful search engines, the Internet is able to provide almost instant feedback on numerous locations worldwide.

RIGHT Climbing on small, local outcrops of rock is a useful way to prepare and get fit for higher climbing trips. Local climbing excursions can, of course, also make for fun adventure outings in their own right.

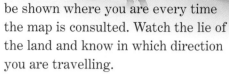

staying alive

The art of survival

Survival can call for some unusual or, perhaps, initially even offensive actions such as trapping animals, eating raw food and bunking down in extremely cramped conditions. The key is to be prepared to do 'whatever it takes' to stay alive.

Although there is generally little room for the niceties of 21st-century civilization when you find yourself in a survival situation, one aspect should always stay firmly in place: that of cooperation with others. You cannot predict when and how you will need the support of your fellow survivors.

Land – practical tips

Land is a more familiar environment than water, so in many ways it is less frightening to be lost in the mountains than suddenly being cast adrift at sea. Nonetheless, survival may call for some irregular techniques such as climbing down a steep rock face. Those who have had occasion to do this will know that it is far more difficult than climbing up. This is an art that can and should be practised, particularly if you frequent steep mountainous areas. The most agile members of a group can help others with vital foot placements from below. In the same way, creating shelter, trapping, finding food, and moving through difficult and unfamiliar territory all require prior practice to be efficient. Cooperation and mutual assistance are necessary to be successful in a survival situation.

In this predicament, shelter is often a major priority. Building some form of shelter as soon as possible can have

the added benefits of helping to attain emotional stability and giving a group something to keep them busy in the early stages after a disaster scenario. Particularly in very cold climates, hypothermia (low body temperature) can be an insidious killer. One often-neglected aspect of survival involves being constantly aware of your surroundings. By keeping an eye on where you are and what is going on around you at all times, you will have useful information in the case of emergencies. Do not rely only on the 'group leader' or 'guide' to follow your group's progress on the map; ask to

be shown where you are every time the map is consulted. Watch the lie of the land and know in which direction you are travelling.

Be sure to make a mental note of noticeable features like rivers, lakes, roads and buildings; and of caves and hollows as possible shelter.

If you are stranded in an entirely unfamiliar area, following a calamity such as an air or train accident, send out one or more scouting parties to look for shelter, food and water as soon as it is feasible to do so without adding to the trauma of the situation.

LEFT A suitable map is essential when planning a trip. Its scale and detail will depend on the type of terrain in which you intend travelling. When you are travelling, refer to your map frequently to avoid getting lost.

BELOW Constructing a snow wall can help to provide group focus in a difficult situation, while the result will make a good wind shelter in subzero temperatures.

Before you undertake any journey into the wilderness in your vehicle, check that it has a spare tyre, that you have the necessary tools to effect minor repairs, that the jack works, that you have snow chains and a shovel and that there is spare fuel, food and water. For a long drive in very cold country, ensure that there is warm clothing in the car – air conditioners and heaters are not much use when you are trapped in a blizzard. Work on the assumption that you might just have to overnight in the car – and pack accordingly.

Water – practical tips

Water is an unfamiliar environment to most people and suddenly finding oneself at the mercy of waves and cold water can be a truly terrifying experience. Keeping the group together after an accident at sea or on a river may well save lives – a group can encourage its weakening members, while a 'survival huddle' can help to preserve warmth and keep members afloat (see picture above). Strong, positive leadership is vital if you wish to initiate and maintain any cooperative formation in the group.

A raft or other flotation device will greatly assist staying alive on water, be it in the sea or when attempting to travel down a tributary in the hope of reaching a major river with some river traffic. Knowledge of ropes, basic knots and lashings is invaluable in creating a temporary flotation device such as a simple raft.

Once again, without being a prophet of gloom, assume that things might go wrong even when undertaking a day

trip out to sea or on a large lake. Pack some extra water and food in waterproof containers and take extra clothing to cope with storms and cold. Check the craft thoroughly beforehand to make sure that it has signalling devices; that the motors, sails and lanyards are sound; that you have sufficient fuel if it is a powerboat; that the bungs are in – leave nothing to chance. If it is not your own craft, don't be shy to ask pertinent safety questions. It is your life, and that of your friends or family.

ABOVE In this survival huddle, an empty plastic container is used to aid flotation. The members of the group can help and encourage each other as strength and resistance waxes and wanes.

LEFT Using an inflatable device makes it easier and much more fun to travel down a river course. Helmet, wet-suit and shoes, however, are essential safety items.

Tactics for survival

A study of numerous survival incidents by the American Rescue Institute has identified certain characteristic common elements of individuals or groups who survive in contrast to those who do not. One of the key factors has been the familiar Boy Scouts' motto: 'Be prepared'. Those who have survived against the odds have not necessarily been the toughest physically, or had the correct equipment. The essence of true survivors has often been mental

tactics *for survival*

readiness to handle unexpected challenges in a survival situation.....

There are many documented feats of incredible endurance – up to 45 days without any food, a week without water, surviving for several days in freezing conditions, epic perseverance in blazing sun. All these grim accounts bear testimony to the hardiness of the human spirit and to the tenacity of those who have clung to life at all costs. In many of these cases, some members of the group have simply given up and let death overtake them, whereas the will to survive has kept others going against all odds.

Survivors in desperate situations have often reported another common factor – one individual or in some cases, a few, had the unshakable optimism that they would be rescued or somehow manage to get themselves out of the situation. This was often associated with a strong faith or religious belief, or with 'something to live for' – a partner and children at home or parents with whom there

After 70 days of being stranded in the Andes mountains, these aeroplane crash survivors resorted to cannabalism.

was a strong bond. By focusing on these factors rather than the 'gloom and doom' of the situation, they enhanced their own and others' chances of survival. The importance of one's mental attitude cannot be over-emphasized – the difference between life and death in a survival situation truly often lies 'in the mind'.

General preparedness

No sane person would launch a business venture without first conducting a great deal of background research and preparation to ensure its viability. Yet a baffling number of people merrily launch out into the wilderness on adventure activities without any form of preparation. The consequences of a failed business enterprise may only entail losing material goods, but those of an adventure trip that goes awry could result in loss of life.

LEFT Maintaining a positive frame of mind is vital in any dire situation. In some cases, help arrives relatively swiftly in the form of a rescue party; in others, an individual or group may need to effect its own salvation. It is necessary to remain calm and objective.

In reality, while it is impossible to ever be 'totally prepared' for anything, you should always make sure that you are as well prepared as time and circumstance allow. By taking the time to simply read a book such as this, you have gone part of the way; by practising some of the skills and improving your fitness you are even better organized; by researching and studying further, you are placing yourself in a position of strength and confidence should you ever need to apply the knowledge.

Personal physical preparedness

Physical fitness is of undeniable value in any outdoor activity. Although it is perhaps not the most important factor in survival, there is no doubt that a fit, healthy person has some advantages over someone who is less physically prepared. Knowingly going into areas where extreme situations might arise – challenging whitewater, high mountain wilderness, polar regions or the Himalaya – without being physically fit is tantamount to idiocy. All too often, people risk their lives rescuing someone who got into difficulties largely as a result of being unfit.

Lashing is a useful skill that should be practised before going on trips.

KEY SURVIVAL PRINCIPLES

QUALITIES OF AN IDEAL LEADER

- Sensitive to group and individual needs, but able to exercise firm control over factors such as food and liquid rationing, allocation of space, clothing and equipment, medical priorities, restrictions on movement and distribution of tasks.
- Able, as far as possible, to make all major decisions in consultation with the group to avoid anyone feeling left out or abandoned (and later becoming a problem due to this isolation, real or imagined).
- Must be flexible, but not vacillating in any decision-making.
- Prepared to hand over leadership either permanently or temporarily under certain circumstances, for example in a medical emergency if one of the party has more medical knowledge, or if a colleague has better mountaineering skills and a steep cliff is encountered.
- Shows confidence and optimism that he or she may not truly feel. Survival can be toughest on the leader.

• BE PREPARED
Preparedness may encompass several forms such as personal physical condition, equipment, activity, advance planning, mental preparedness, leadership factors and knowledge of survival strategies. (For details see pp 18–19.)

• PRACTISE ESSENTIAL SKILLS
Practice makes perfect — many difficult skills such as lashings, firemaking and navigation will not be of much value unless you practise them enough to be confident in using them. If you are insecure in their application under ideal conditions, how much worse is it going to be in a howling gale, with cold, hungry, injured party members depending on you? On their own, these constitute fun activities that can liven up a hiking trip or provide an entertaining afternoon in the comfort of your local woods next to your favourite fishing hole.

Why not plan a family, club or scout troop survival weekend, complete with fire-making, building shelter, some navigation exercises and primitive fishing and food gathering (perhaps with a little emergency canned food hidden away in the car boot in case you need it.)

• ASSESS THE SITUATION
Avoiding panic, pausing to evaluate the resources of the situation and the group, and examining your options are essential before adopting a course of action.

Every survival situation is unique — there will be a novel mix of people, a specific set of conditions, a different amount of equipment.

However, there will usually be common threads running through all incidents, with optimal ways of solving problems.

The normal skills of everyday modern life become largely meaningless, and decisions have to be made about unfamiliar circumstances. It becomes very difficult to predict the outcomes, and conventional logic often seems irrelevant.

• ADAPT OR DIE
Clear thinking and an appraisal of the situation is needed. The ability to adapt methods and patterns to accommodate new and unusual circumstances becomes vital.

The party or individual may have to adapt to new ideas on movement patterns, food, clothing, water use, independence and leadership, to name but a few.

Modern urban man has lost touch with his natural environment and is generally ill-equipped to deal with the harsh realities of nature without his comfort zone of pre-prepared food, water on tap, convenience clothing and mechanical and electrical devices. Yet man is also a survivor by nature, and the basic instincts of 'fight or flight' are there to stand you in good stead if you can conquer your fear of the unknown long enough to use them.

Every single item or situation has to be evaluated in a new way and questions need to be asked. How can I use this piece of equipment? Should I take it along or leave it behind? What benefit can this item be to me? Nothing should be taken for granted.

preparedness

ABOVE Training to raise fitness levels before a trip is important and can be tailored to a specific routine.

Part of physical fitness is ensuring that certain health basics are taken care of before a long trip – dental problems, a routine medical check-up, any nagging ailments, sprained muscles or ligament injuries. Have all recommended inoculations (e.g. hepatitis A, tetanus and yellow fever) and purchase prophylactic medicines (i.e. anti-malarial drugs) before your trip. The rest of your physical preparedness involves appropriate exercise – aerobics, weight training, running, cycling, rowing. If necessary, consult a reputable and experienced personal trainer or fitness consultant to work out a suitable training programme aimed at improving your general level of fitness and focus on any specialized fitness requirements you may need.

Activity preparedness

Proper preparation for negotiating a trackless desert might include extensive 4x4 driving courses and motor maintenance; sea kayaking needs expertise in handling waves, swells and currents; climbing needs knowledge of techniques and equipment. Each activity has certain skills that need to be honed before one is competent enough to attempt difficult ventures. Don't hesitate to consult experts for coaching and advice before your trip. A flooded river is not the place to learn how to eskimo roll in a canoe, and fumbling with unfamiliar knots in a whiteout storm is not the wisest move when you are perched on a 6000m (20,000ft) peak.

Mental preparedness

Of all the aspects of survival, the mind is probably the most important. People who have survived against all odds have been those who wanted to survive with every fibre of their being. Most creatures have this instinct for survival – in his book *The Selfish Gene*, Richard Dawkins postulates that it is this very essence of man's genetic makeup that makes us wish to perpetuate ourselves, our subgroup and our species. But it is likely that only man can rationalize survival and consciously decide to give up or go on. The survivors are those who are mentally prepared to give their all and never give in. Mental toughness is what true survival is all about. Fight the doubts, fight the tendency to say 'I will never make it' – focus instead on the incredible survival records of others – if they did it, so can you.

Leadership

Any group has individuals with various strengths and weaknesses and is subject to a conflict of personalities that can rip the group apart and reduce the chances of survival. Firm but tactful leadership can be essential in tough survival situations, particularly in the initial stages after a disaster. Depression, hopelessness, recklessness and confusion can all take their toll, mentally and physically. If a natural competent leader does not emerge, it is wise for the group to democratically elect a 'captain' as soon as possible. It has been amply proven that even poor leadership under extreme conditions is better than no leadership at all.

Knowledge of survival strategies

Even for someone with the absolute minimum of equipment, all is not lost. The knowledge of survival tricks and strategies and the will to survive are powerful tools. Simply reading manuals such as this gives you an advantage in the survival stakes while any practice you may have undertaken strengthens your hand immeasurably. Perhaps the best survival strategy is the one that is often forgotten – STOP and THINK. A carefully worked out, logical solution is more likely to succeed than a spur-of-the-moment 'quick fix'.

Advance and contingency planning

Information is another vital key – the more facts you have on the area, the better prepared you are for survival. Make a point of finding out about the people, their lifestyles, customs and taboos; anticipated weather patterns; heights and topography of hills and mountains; river flow; vegetation; edible and inedible plants; animal life; ocean currents and water temperatures. The Internet and books offer a wealth of information, as do travellers who have already visited a particular area. Be sure to take along up-to-date maps, guide books and books on fauna and flora. Carefully plan the entire trip with your group before leaving. Any delays or disasters will be so much easier to handle if the responsibility is shared and you can tap your companions' knowledge.

LEFT Undeterred by his blindness, climber John Dove is guided by a fellow mountaineer in the Bernese Alps, Switzerland. It is this sort of tenacious determination that forms the essence of survival.

RIGHT Mountaineers on Mount Tarawera, New Zealand, listen carefully to their leader's briefing.

planning

Delegate responsibilities to different team members, such as food planning, route mapping, equipment collection and emergency contingencies. Decide beforehand who will be the quartermaster, the cook, the navigator, mechanic, medic and leader.

These roles should, however, be flexible. It is wise for each group member to be able to assume another role and responsibility as this will help spread the organizer's load. Ensure that each member leaves pertinent details such as the scheduling, dates, list of participants and contact details with their next of kin in case of an emergency.

Making contingency plans

Things seldom go totally according to plan. Depending on the nature of the excursion, various advance contingency plans need to be put in place.
Plan your schedule: for all trips, especially those in back country, the wilderness and at sea, have an expected departure and trip completion times and projected contact plans. If the scheduled contacts are not adhered to, your contact person(s) should be instructed to notify the relevant authorities and should be given clear instructions on what steps to take.
Route plan: Leave a projected trip plan with a suitable contact person or with the relevant authorities such as forestry, mountain rescue, the harbour master, coastguard, or aviation control if you are undertaking a private flight of any nature.
Emergency escape routes: If you are planning a long hike in mountains or

an extended river trip, it is important to plot several emergency escape routes on the route card (see p160). Remember to always leave a copy with your contact person. In the case of injury, illness or bad weather causing delays, this will help rescuers narrow their search options.
Regrouping plan: If you are going hiking, skiing or canoeing in back-country areas, make clear plans both beforehand and on a daily or even hourly basis for regrouping or other action in case your group becomes separated or one of the members goes missing.

Commercial adventure operators

A common scenario is a group or an individual contracting a guide or a trekking operator to lead them on an adventure experience – be it hiking, rafting, climbing, canoeing or other organized outdoor adventure. While there are some excellent commercial operators with flawless records and impeccable operating procedures, others fly close to the wind and can put their group at risk. Sadly, there

An organized expedition through acacia country in Mali, near Timbuktu. A convoy of similar vehicles will minimize the spares and tyres that have to be carried.

are numerous examples of deaths and disasters resulting largely if not solely from operator incompetence. It is worth your while to shop around and do your homework thoroughly on adventure operators before you consider using their services. If necessary, ask for recommendations from others who have used commercial operators. You could also ask the operator for some references and the names of previous clients whom you could contact directly.

Political considerations

Many areas of the world are subject to sudden political and/or religious turmoil, or even outright warfare, with little prior warning for the unwary adventure traveller. Local factions do not often have any real interest in involving foreigners in their disputes and by being circumspect you can avoid trouble.

WHAT TO LOOK FOR IN AN OPERATOR

You would not put your life in the hands of a doctor for a critical operation unless you had done some research on him — place your adventure operator under the same scrutiny. Insist on being provided with pertinent information. Only when you are satisfied with the answers should you make use of any operator's services.

- What is their track record?
- How long has the company been operating?
- Is your proposed trip one that is regularly offered by the operator?
- Does the operator use only qualified and experienced guides?
- Does the operator carry public liability insurance? (This is a good way of establishing an operator's reliable and solid track record, since only established companies can obtain and afford public liability under normal circumstances.)
- Which authority issued the operator's credentials - national body or similar?
- What is their equipment like? (Ask to see it if necessary.)
- Does the operator have contingency plans in the event of an emergency or accident? If so, ask them to specify.

Coping with hostile behaviour

- Avoid sudden hand movements, particularly into a bag, your vehicle or pockets — these could well be misinterpreted as an attempt to reach for a weapon.
- Make a submissive gesture, such as palms up, hands forward, head slightly bowed to symbolize 'I have no weapon, and am not a threat'. Avoid aggressive eye contact and any form of verbal argument or confrontation. Remain quiet and respectful, even if the demands seem unreasonable.
- Avoid wearing expensive clothes or flashy jewellery and do not openly display money, pricy cameras and watches. In many of the world's poorer countries such items may represent more wealth than the country's average citizen could hope to possess in a lifetime.
- If someone is determined to take your possessions, even after you have quietly but firmly refused, hand them over. Your life should always take precedence over material possessions.
- Respect local dress and cultural or religious codes of conduct (e.g. covering the head, women refraining from wearing shorts, not drinking in public). It usually does not pay to antagonize local residents.
- Waiting may constitute part of the process – impatience is noticed and seldom appreciated by those who deem themselves to be 'in charge'. Some things just cannot be hurried. This seems to be true of many passport authorities in particular – petty border-post officials like to wield a great deal of power in order to delay, confiscate your goods or even imprison you.
- Never shout and gesticulate. Rather be as calm, undemanding and friendly as the circumstances allow. By curbing your impatience and annoyance, and showing firmness well tempered by respect, you may survive a situation that might otherwise spiral out of your control.
- Do not take photographs of military installations, government buildings or security forces.
- You can usually achieve far more by cooperation than by confrontation in hostile encounters.
- Do not make, or respond positively towards derogatory comments about the country's government, current leader or those in authority, even if you think that the locals may agree with you.
- Ensure that all legal medicines are properly boxed, with full and appropriate labelling. NEVER carry drugs and avoid carrying liquor, especially in Muslim countries.
- Carry a 'sacrificial bank roll' in an accessible pocket or pouch where it can be easily reached. Your main cash and travel documents should be carried hidden in a thin pouch under your clothing.

BASIC KIT

BASIC KIT

There are essentially two kinds of survival situations: those that occur without warning during an everyday activity – such as an aeroplane trip that turns into a disaster when it crashes in inaccessible terrain – and unintentional mishaps that occur when a person or group takes part in a planned outdoor activity. In the former, one is unlikely to be carrying any form of substantial survival kit; in the latter, where there is a likelihood of potential problems that may result in a survival situation, it is always wise to be well prepared by including certain items or an entire survival kit in your personal or group luggage.

Normal hiking kit

Most multi-day hikes require a basic set of gear such as a sleeping bag and groundsheet (or a tent), clothing, eating utensils and food. It takes experience of several trips before you discover the optimal collection of hiking and camping gear. It is highly recommended that even on day hikes, you should have items such as raincoats, water bottles, a warm top, long trousers, a first-aid kit, a lamp and some food.

Personal kit

The first item in your personal kit is a backpack. Choose your pack carefully from the wide selection available. A backpack should be appropriate to your body size, hold all the items you need to take along, and above all, be durable and comfortable. For any hike longer than a few hours' duration, it is vital to have a well-padded hip belt that helps to stabilize and hold the weight of your pack, thus relieving pressure on your shoulders. Apart from normal hiking gear, each member should also have the following equipment:

Head lamp: A compact but powerful head lamp makes travelling in bush or steep terrain safer. Take along spare batteries and bulbs. Make sure that the lamp cannot switch on accidentally and therefore deplete the batteries.

Raincoat: A good raincoat is

Head lamp

essential and can provide insulation in cold or windy conditions. It is preferable to choose one with a drawstring-type hood. Some raincoats, made from high-quality 'breathable' fabric, keep you drier than standard plastic raincoats because they allow perspiration to pass through.

Water bottle: Even in areas with good water supplies, it is always wise to carry a full bottle – particularly if the water you find might have to be purified before use.

Warm clothing: Do not be caught unprepared by changing weather conditions. Tracksuit pants, a warm top and a balaclava are advised for most hikes.

Survival pouch

On hikes or multi-day trips a larger survival pouch on your backpack would usually contain a mini survival kit. The survival items in this kit can fit into a small tin or other waterproof container that can be easily carried in a pocket or pouchbag when venturing into the wilderness. For frequent aeroplane travellers who like to be prepared, a mini survival kit could easily fit into a jacket or briefcase side pocket.

Mini medical kit

This kit should comprise basic medical supplies and some clearly labelled basic tablets packaged in plastic.

Analgesic: (e.g. Paracetamol – Acetaminophen in the USA) and/or codeine phosphate.
Anti-diarrhoea medication: e.g. Loperamide (Immodium®)
Antihistamine: e.g. Promethazine (Phenergan®) – for insect bites, stings, allergies etc.
Latex gloves: crepe bandage and a sterile wound dressing should be included if space allows.

Personal mini survival kit

Plastic bag: Choose a strong one to carry or to collect water in a still.
Flexible (wire) saw: This is useful as it can even cut large branches. Coat with grease and keep in a plastic bag.

Surgical blade: For cutting off dead skin or a multitude of other uses.
Fish hooks: Choose ones that are intended for small- to medium-sized fish (e.g. gauge 5). Include a few small, pea-sized sinkers.
Wire: Thin wire (e.g. brass picture wire) is useful for making snares and many other tasks such as fixing shoes.
Button compass: Buy one that is preferably luminous and check on it regularly as small compasses are prone to rust.
Candle: This is used to start a fire rather than as a light source.
Magnifying glass: Vital for starting tinder fires or to make splinter removal easier.
Safety pins: These perform various fastening functions and can also double as fish hooks.
Waterproof matches: These are either bought as such, or standard matches can be waterproofed by dipping them in hot candle wax.
Flint: This often has a magnesium block with it to aid fire lighting. Shavings from the block usually flare up easily when lit.
Butterfly sutures: Invaluable for holding a wound together.
Needle and thread: Used to repair clothes, sleeping bags etc.
Plasters: Preferably waterproof and in many different sizes.

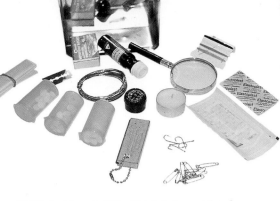

ABOVE A mini survival kit, which includes a mini medical kit, can be fitted into a small, robust tin.

ABOVE A well-organized method of packing compartments of a backpack ensure easy accessibility.

This little pouch can be kept in a separate, bigger survival bag.

Water bottles come in different shapes.

Warm jacket

Raincoat

group kit

Survival kit for groups

The group should have at least one of the following items:

Compass: A good compass preferably with a luminous dial (e.g. the Silva-type or Polaris compass) is an essential back country tool.

Maps: A reliable topographical map (to a scale of 1 : 50,000 or more detailed) should be laminated or carried in a waterproof pouch.

Stove and fuel: Gas stoves are the easiest and most reliable to use. Those with detachable cartridges are generally the safest. Use propane-butane fuel for higher altitudes.

Water purification tablets: To purify

natural water before use. Remember that few water sources are unpolluted.

First-aid kit: This should contain plasters, bandages, antiseptic cream, scissors, forceps, latex gloves and certain basic medicines (see p124).

A pack or two of playing cards may seem an unusual item to include in a group hiking kit. However, cards could prove a useful diversion if you find yourself in a survival predicament. Delays or survival situations lead to long periods of waiting that can fray nerves and impose additional stress on a group. Other activities

such as word games and charades are important if there are children in the group – should there be a survival situation it could help to calm them and take their minds off the emergency at hand.

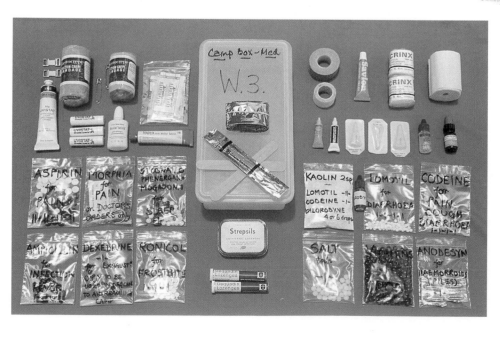

TOP CENTRE Not just entertainment – games, quizzes and discussions are an invaluable diversion to reduce stress when waiting for rescue or a chance to move.

ABOVE LEFT Detachable compact gas burner; multifuel stove; detachable high-output gas burner.

ABOVE CENTRE A selection of fuel bottles and compact gas cylinders. The right-hand bottle is clearly marked as 'fuel'; the others should also be marked before use. Take careful note of instructions on gas cylinders before attaching or detaching from the burner.

ABOVE Maps and a compass are essential group items.

LEFT Remember medicines for common travel illnesses. To save space, remove contents from original containers, then clearly mark the name and usage instructions on the plastic bags.

Environment-specific gear

Back country

'Back country' or wilderness is an accepted term for any 'wild', natural countryside. The items listed for this kind of trip are best carried on the person in secure pockets or a hip pouch, or in a daypack or hiking bag. The very best option might be to pack all the items into a watertight mess tin and then carry that in a single 'survival pouch'. This kit could quite easily be transferred to a vehicle, aeroplane, canoe, or hiking pack, depending on the circumstances.

Pouch: A compact, waterproof pouch made from strong material with a solid fastening is ideal.

Mess tin: This helps to protect certain items and also doubles as a cooking utensil. The best form is thin stainless steel or aluminium with a fold-away handle. If polished it also serves as a useful signalling mirror.

Pocket knife: It takes much to beat the small, multi-bladed Swiss Army knife, although a strong durable

multi-purpose tool (e.g. Leatherman®) is more useful as it has the advantage of including a pair of pliers.

Solid fuel tablets: The fuel should accompany a small fold-away stove or potholder. Fuel tablets can also be used as fire lighters.

Small pocket lighter: A lighter can be even more useful than matches in wet or windy conditions. It is very important to replace or maintain lighters regularly as they tend to rust and can leak.

Thin, straw-sized plastic tube; about 50cm (18in) long: Useful as a straw for obtaining water from various sources or as a tourniquet.

Lamp: A small, waterproof lamp with a set of spare batteries and bulb. It helps to turn one of the batteries in the lamp around to prevent it from switching on accidentally.

Whistle: The piercing sound of a plastic whistle can assist searchers in finding you.
(Avoid metal whistles – they rust in the sea and can freeze onto your lips in very cold conditions.)

Food essentials: Handy sachets of tea, sugar, milk powder and instant soup can be lifesavers.

Energy boosters: Slabs of chocolate

and/or glucose sweets are valuable energy sources.

Plastic bags: Any excess space should be taken up with a strong plastic sheet or bag, which can double as a poncho or survival bag if necessary.

Notebook and pencil: For creating maps or for sending/leaving messages.

Flares: Mini flares are very practical, particularly if heading into the sea or remote back country. A group should take at least one set. Flares should be handled carefully and MUST NOT be used once they have passed their expiry date. They can be bought in good waterproof containers.

Mini survival kit: This kit (see p25) should be packed into the larger survival pouch or carried on your person.

ABOVE The multi-purpose Leatherman® is invaluable.
BELOW A selection of rescue flares and equipment (clockwise from centre top): chemical light stick, distress rocket, white marker flare, mini flares in waterproof container, smoke flare, hand held marker flare. Follow instructions for use carefully, and use only when you are sure searchers can see them.

mountain gear

Mountains

In addition to the very basic camping kit that has already been mentioned, anyone planning to travel in high, mountainous areas or cold, snow-filled regions needs specialized kit to cope in a survival situation.

Personal mountain kit

Ice axe: This is an essential tool for walking in ice-covered terrain with slopes that are more than very gently angled. A long walking axe is all that is needed for mountaineering not involving near-vertical slopes – terrain that is best left to specialist mountaineers. Fasten the axe securely to your belt or harness with a leash so that it cannot be lost if dropped.

Ski poles: When walking on snow and ice or traversing rough terrain, particularly on a downhill, ski poles are often more useful than a long ice axe. They help to prevent pressure on the knees.

Warm fleece clothing: This should be worn according to the principle of layering (see p39).

Lined parka jacket: A hooded rainproof parka will prevent the loss of body heat.

Balaclava: This reduces the potentially considerable heat loss from the head.

Gloves: Many climbers wear several pairs of this important accessory – thin inner gloves, then thicker fleece or woollen mitts, covered by good-quality waterproof outer gloves.

Sturdy boots: Boots should be waterproof (Gore-Tex®-lined ones are a good choice) and be able to accommodate your foot with at least two pairs of warm *socks*.

Gaiters: This handy cloth or nylon covering will help to keep snow out of the top of boots.

Overtrousers: Wind- and waterproof trousers or salopettes (quilted trousers held up by shoulder straps), are effective in keeping the legs dry and warm.

Sleeping bag: A very warm sleeping bag is a must. Down-filled types are warmer and lighter, but they compact into useless balls when wet. Synthetic fill is bulkier, but dries out relatively fast and retains its special insulating properties even after getting wet.

Foam insulating mat: A useful base to place under the sleeping bag.

Sunglasses: Essential eye protection against glaring UV light at altitude, they also prevent snow-blindness.

Group mountain kit

This will vary immensely according to the nature of the mountains but will generally include a good climbing rope and some slings, as well as very specialized rock- or ice-climbing gear. Novices and inexperienced adventurers should not experiment in this terrain and must venture out only if accompanied by an expert.

Ice axe

Ski poles

ABOVE A climber dressed for high-altitude climbing sports many layers of clothing to keep warm, and gaiters to prevent snow from sliding into the top of her boots. Note also the pouch containing personal survival gear, and good-quality sunglasses to protect the eyes.

BELOW Even for moderately dressed climbers who go adventuring along lower mountain slopes, a modicum of safety equipment and warm clothing is advisable, as weather conditions are often unpredictable.

Caving adventures

Although caving is a popular pastime, it holds many dangers for the novice. Most people are unaccustomed to scrambling up or down in limited light and it is difficult to detect drop-offs or water with the interplay of light and shadow created by lamps. One should never attempt complex, difficult caves (i.e. those with many branched passages or levels) without considerable experience. No cave that requires ropework in the entrance, exit or any part of the route should be entered without trained guides and suitable equipment.

Personal caving kit

Clothing: If you envisage doing any crawling, wear sturdy trousers and a long-sleeved shirt. Tough boots or shoes are useful. As caves are seldom very cold, bulky jerseys are usually more of a hindrance than help; however, thin, warmish clothing such as polypropylene undergarments beneath an overall are ideal.

Helmet: A hard head covering is recommended to avoid bumping your head or sustaining injuries from small stones that may be dislodged by climbers above you. An alternative is to wear a woollen cap or felt hat for protection. Avoid hats with large rims as they prevent you from seeing what is happening above you.

Lamp: A head lamp is best to allow hands-free movement. Fasten it to the helmet with duct tape if it does not have a suitable strap. Do not stint on the quality and price of a lamp – reliable access to light in a dark cave environment is all-important.

Spare lamp: Each member of the group should ensure that they carry a good-quality spare lamp to cope with emergency situations.

Batteries and bulbs: Each person should carry at least one (preferably two) spare sets of batteries and a spare bulb. The latter can often be taped inside the lamp head or body.

Food and water: A small amount of food such as chocolate, energy bars and dried fruit are welcome and vital nourishment during a hard day's caving. Always remember to carry a full water bottle.

Pack: It is useful to take a small, tough pack or slingbag in which to carry spare food and water.

Group caving kit

Spare lamp(s): You have to have light in the dark interior of a cave. Many groups land in an unpleasant predicament when their only light source fails. Take at least one spare lamp, batteries and bulbs per group.

Candles and matches: This is useful both for emergency light and to mark your return route. Take care to remove all traces of candlewax or matches and do not place lit candles where they can ruin sensitive dripstone formations.

Compass, paper and pencil: These are vital for keeping track of turns and directions taken while exploring caves. They can then be used for backtracking.

Rope: Use proper 'static' caving rope, which is made of material that is less susceptible to battery chemicals than normal climbing rope. This is useful to safeguard cavers on moderate, short slopes or tied around ankles to back-haul in tight passages. (Cave roping is a highly specialized pursuit and should only be attempted by those who are familiar with its technique.)

Strong string or nylon cord: Useful to mark your way in complex underground passages. Ensure that the string is securely tied at the start and remove it when exiting the cave.

First-aid kit: Take a kit to be able to cope with minor abrasions and scratches.

Head lamps and flashlights provide vital light in dark caves like the one above.

desert gear

Desert essentials

Travel in hot, arid areas needs specialized clothing and a suitable vehicle that is carefully packed with certain basic essentials.

Personal desert kit

Clothing: This should be lightweight cotton, loose-fitting and light-coloured to reflect heat. Long-sleeved shirts and long trousers will prevent undue exposure to the sun.

T-shirt: This helps to keep the body cool by absorbing and dissipating perspiration from the skin.

Hat: A broad-brimmed hat aids ventilation and keeps the sun off the head.

Sunglasses: A good-quality pair of sunglasses filters out UVA and UVB rays and prevents eye-strain in the harsh reflective glare of the desert.

Jacket: A warm, windproof jacket is needed as desert temperatures can drop drastically at night.

Sunscreen: A sunblock cream with a sun protection factor (SPF) of 20 or even higher helps to protect the skin from painful sunburn.

Group desert kit

Extra water: Any vehicle travelling through a desert area (even on good roads) should carry adequate emergency rations of water in case of a breakdown or accident. Carry the water in multiple containers rather than one large one to avoid losing your entire supply due to leakage or contamination with oil or other unpalatable substances.

Plastic sail or groundsheet: This can be used to create shade during the day and for extra warmth at night. Ground sheets can also be very useful to collect water through condensation or to make 'stills' from plants.

Vehicle spares: Tyres, tools, and basic engine spares must be packed. Extra fuel, as well as a fanbelt, radiator hose, fuses and other parts (e.g. spark plugs, points and a condenser) should be carried for trips to remote wilderness areas away from 'civilization'.

Food: Carry provisions that will last at least three days in the vehicle.

ABOVE A sensibly dressed desert explorer.

TOP LEFT A broad-spectrum sunscreen lotion should have an SPF of 20 or higher.

ABOVE LEFT (Water canteens, clockwise from top): a small bottle suitable for day hikes; bottle with sip tube; larger version for extended hiking; 'Camelbak' container for longer adventure trips.

BELOW Create shade with a groundsheet. Rocks placed above your head should be stable in case of wind.

Machete

jungle gear

Jungles and tropical areas

Jungles and tropical rainforests can be difficult to move through. The dense tangle of vegetation snares you and makes progress laboured, the atmosphere is uncomfortably humid and there is the prospect of encountering various insects and reptiles.

In these conditions, heat exhaustion poses as much of a threat as hypothermia does in cold areas – dehydration can be an unexpected hazard. Counter this by carrying plenty of liquid.

Clothing: This is essentially the same as for desert conditions, but tougher material is preferable.

Drawstring trousers: These help to keep leeches and other crawling creatures out (elastic bands can be used).

Mosquito-net fringe on hat: This vital fringe can be fitted when needed, in the evening or when resting.

Machete or large knife: This broad, heavy knife is very useful when cutting away vegetation.

Insect repellent: This item is a must and should be applied to hands, arms and other exposed body parts. Avoid the forehead and around the eyes, as perspiration will sting the eyes..

Anti-malarial medication: Many tropical and subtropical areas are plagued by malaria-carrying (*anopheles*) mosquitoes. Do not disregard the warnings issued by health authorities. Be sure to check with your doctor or a clinic before you visit any affected regions, and let them advise you on suitable options.

Medical kit: Injuries rapidly become infected in the tropics. Prevent any infections by covering wounds with a sterile, waterproof dressing and ensure that you have anti-fungal cream for your feet.

Mosquito net: Suspended over your bed at night, this is a highly effective way to protect yourself against being bitten by mosquitoes.

ABOVE Waterproof shoes will keep your feet dry, while drawstring trousers prevent leeches from getting in.

LEFT A net that can be attached to a hat is invaluable in mosquito-ridden regions.

RIGHT Insect repellents, vital in many areas, are available in the form of candles, creams, lotions or sprays.

sea & diving gear

Sea voyages

Ocean-going vessels are required by law to carry certain basic rescue and emergency gear, which includes life rafts (or life jackets on smaller craft), radio, flares, and often rescue beacons. Certain items such as life rafts are indispensable when venturing into rough or potentially stormy waters. It is also valuable to have a comprehensive Survival Kit (see p25) in an easily accessible pouch.

Check that any craft you are sailing in has these basic emergency stores and know where to find them:
Raft or dinghy: These are usually easily inflatable and should be made of tough canvas or rubber. They must be stable, have plenty of places to hold on to and preferably have some form of built-in shelter. Ensure that there is basic survival gear (including water) on board.
Flares: Both parachute flares and red hand-held or smoke flares greatly assist your chances of being seen by rescuers. (Check that expiry dates are still valid.)
Strobe lights: Powerful, compact strobe lights are easily visible at night and can even be fastened onto individual life jackets.
Waterproof containers: These are used to hold vital personal effects, as well as emergency rations, waterproof matches, maps and flares.
Sea anchor (drogue): This can be streamed behind the boat to keep the bows facing into the direction of the weather and restrict drifting.
Gaff and net: Invaluable for catching fish in extended survival conditions. Keep the gaff point embedded in

A store-bought and an improvised gaff, with a small net. Any experienced fisherman will tell you that landing the fish you have hooked is half the battle.

cork or similar to avoid damaging the craft or injuring one of its occupants.
Cord: Strong nylon cord has many uses in shipboard survival.

Diving trips

A scuba diver will usually have an inflatable Buoyancy Compensator (BC) that has a whistle attached to it. This specialized 'life jacket' holds the scuba cylinder and can be inflated from it, or by mouth. It is used to control a diver's buoyancy and is usually fully inflated on the surface to keep the diver high in the water.

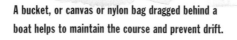

A bucket, or canvas or nylon bag dragged behind a boat helps to maintain the course and prevent drift.

ABOVE This scuba diver is well-prepared for any emergencies as she is carrying all the correct gear necessary for safe diving.

Some useful items to aid survival and rescue which can easily be stowed in the pouch of the BC are:
Signal buoy or surface-marker buoy: This can be inflated by mouth or by using air from the diving cylinder. It projects far enough above the surface to make the diver visible to boats.
Strobe light: Small, compact but very bright, this light is easily visible at night and even attracts attention in the daytime.
Waterproofed mini flares: These can be seen from a long distance, particularly at night.

Using vehicles and spare parts

In the event of a serious accident in which a vehicle is wrecked or rendered unusable, many parts can be used in the ensuing survival situation. Great care should be taken if there is still fuel in any tank(s), or if parts of the vehicle are likely to collapse and injure those inside. If there is any sign of spilt fuel, wait until the vehicle has cooled down completely. The first priority may be to make the vehicle interior suitable for shelter; always be aware of the dangers of fuel, other combustible material and exposed electric wiring.

Note that many synthetic fabrics such as seat covers and cushions, as well as plastic mouldings, give off poisonous fumes as they burn or smoulder. Stripping and abandoning a vehicle may be a tough decision to have to make, and should only be considered if it truly outweighs the benefits of staying in or near it. Vehicles are bigger and, therefore, usually more easily visible than people in air searches. If you do decide to move away from the vehicle, carefully consider what can be removed and taken along to your advantage.

ABOVE Many vehicle parts can be used, such as this air filter, which can make a useful cup or scoop after rinsing it clean.

LEFT ABOVE A stiff floor mat can be rolled into an effective splint, or used to handle warm objects, or for additional insulation in cold regions.

FAR LEFT A hubcap becomes a water container, pot, or a spade. Ingenuity is the key.

USEFUL VEHICLE PARTS

- Hubcaps make good pots and water carriers.
- Mirrors can be used for signalling.
- Tyres cut into pieces can make tough hardy sandal soles and can also be used effectively for fuel and for signal smoke.
- Inner tubes are useful water carriers although the water may subsequently not taste too good. They can also be used as flotation devices across rivers, fuel, slingshot bands, elastic bandages and for carrying loads.
- Radiators have a good water supply, however: DO NOT DRINK WATER FROM ANY RADIATOR THAT MAY HAVE CONTAINED ANTI-FREEZE, EVEN AFTER DISTILLATION. MANY CONTAIN ETHYLENE GLYCOL, WHICH IS HIGHLY POISONOUS. Radiator fluid can be used for cooling stills or cleaning items.

- Grease or oil can be used to light fires and can also be smeared on as a deterrent against mosquitoes and other insects.
- Battery and light can be used for nighttime signals. The battery is also useful to start fires, or to power radios, cellphones etc. Be sure not to overload the battery's voltage limit.
- Tools (e.g. screwdrivers) can make very handy weapons, as well as digging and hunting tools.
- Roofracks/ladders/bonnets/cargo mats can be used as sledges and to transport goods or injured group members.
- Air filters make a good stove base if they are one of the metal-framed models, while some can even be used as a pre-filter in purifying water.

- Seat covers can be used as additional cover, for straining liquids, and as bandages and supports in first aid situations.
- Window glass is a useful signalling device, the larger the better, to attract attention.
- Seats and carpets can be used to create shelter 'tunnels', or for insulation as a groundsheet.
- Electrical flex is effective as a fishing line, for starting fires (see p73) and for tying or fastening objects.
- Maps and charts may give some indication where you are and which way to go if movement is your best option.

A sun shield can act as reflector for fires, and as a 'space blanket'; fan belts make tough slings; air filters pre-filter water; electrical wire is used as a cord.

basic tools

Basic tools

Tools in survival situations generally take the place of knives, hammers or saws. In some cases, they may even become hunting implements or be used as weapons.

If planning carefully, you will take some store-bought items along with you on your outing.

Penknife: A sharp, strong penknife (folding-blade knife) is a valuable tool. Keep it attached to your belt or your body with a lanyard. The authentic Swiss Army knives are both tough and versatile as they have many useful blades, including screwdrivers, saws, and awls (a pointed tool with a fluted blade for piercing wood). Some versions even have built-in scissors and tweezers.

Sheath knife: A strong sheath knife (fixed-blade knife) is indispensable in the wild; choose one that has a solid tang going right through the handle as this can be used even if the wooden or plastic handle breaks. It is always a good idea to have a sheath that holds the knife securely and has a loop for a belt.

Survival knife: Some experts prefer a hollow-handled style of knife, which can carry some survival kit and easily be turned into a spear. If you do choose one of these, make sure it is a strong one. Any large, sharp knife with a serrated piece for a sawblade is also suitable. A robust sheath with an effective clip protects the knife and prevents it being lost.

Kukri, parang or machete: These are all large, heavy powerful hybrids between a knife and an axe, used for hunting, cutting wood and clearing away vegetation. The kukri is the traditional tool of the Nepalese, while the parang is used in Malaysia. Machetes are used worldwide in bush or jungle areas and are extremely useful. The weight and size of the machete blade makes it as effective as an axe for felling small trees.

Axe: If you are lucky enough to have an axe, treat it with care – it is one of the most valuable tools in the bush.

Multi-purpose tools: Multi-blade tools such as Leatherman® fulfil a host of functions as they feature solid blades, useful pliers and saws. These multi-purpose devices are well worth the investment and no serious adventure traveller should be without one.

Making utensils

Tools can be created from diverse sources including glass, metal or the tough plastic parts of vehicles. Before leaving a vehicle, make sure that you have stripped it of all useful parts.

Creating tools

This guideline indicates the type of tools you can make if you find yourself in a survival situation.

Stone tools: Prehistoric man made efficient tools from bone, stone and other natural objects. This is not as easy as it sounds but can be done with persistence and practice. To create stone tools, split flakes off a large, solid piece of rock with softer stones (for smaller, finer flakes use hard pieces of wood or bone). Heavy smooth black rock such as flint or obsidian makes good tools. Stone tools can be used as scrapers, knives, spear points, arrowheads or axeheads.

Wooden tools: A simple but effective tool or weapon is a wooden spear – whittle the end of a 2m (6ft) hardwood pole, then temper (harden) the point with a few seconds of repeated cooling and heating in a fire, rotating the point while you do this.

Glass knife: A shard of glass wrapped in leather or cloth can be a very effective tool, particularly for gutting fish or other animals. To make one from a bottle, wrap the bottle thoroughly in cloth, then tap it firmly on a hard surface. Open the cloth, watching for sharp shards of glass. Select a long piece with a sharp edge and thick base for a handle. A robust covering on the handle section is essential to prevent injury to the user. Tie this on with tape, string or other suitable alternative.

TOP A multi-purpose Swiss Army knife.

LEFT A shard of glass makes a useful cutting tool, but be sure to bind one end.

BELOW Prehistoric man shaped various effective cutting tools from bone and stone.

Bamboo knife: Bamboo can be made into an effective tool or hunting spear for smaller animals or a shovel for digging out roots and bulbs. Cut a long section of bamboo at one end at an angle to create a point. If you have no knife, break bamboo by snapping it over a tree branch until you get a suitable sharp end. Sharpen it further by rubbing it on a rough surface.

A piece of bamboo, sharpened to a point at one end, can be affixed to a stick and used as spear.

Slingshot: Easier to make than a catapult, but this David-and-Goliath weapon is far more difficult to use. All you need is a piece of leather (or even tough cloth) for the pouch and two lengths of rope or twine for the thongs. Make a hole in each side of the pouch and attach the thongs. Smooth stones work best in this slingshot.

The key to using a slingshot effectively is to work up a good speed when twirling it above your head, then release one thong in the correct direction. Make sure you have no one near you when trying out your slingshot, as your direction will be unpredictable

for a good number of attempts. Slingshots are capable of killing large animals.

Catapults: A catapult is most useful in catching small game such as birds, rodents and even small buck. Use hard, solid wood or tough greenish wood to make the V-shaped handle; an inner tube makes superb elastic, and a piece of leather (your wallet, or the tongue of your shoe) the pouch. River pebbles are generally the best ammunition; another option is to use ball bearings from your vehicle

Throwing stick: The simplest of all weapons can be a throwing stick or simply a stone, which can be surprisingly efficient. In extreme survival situations that call for killing game and birds, these might produce good results.

Choose or cut a solid, moderately heavy stick about .5m (1½ft) long, preferably one with a small knob (e.g. a truncated branch) on the end.

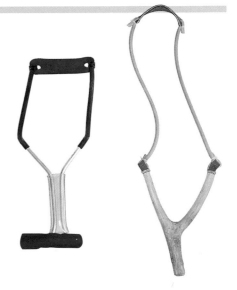

ABOVE A powerful store-bought hunting catapult (left) and the more humble homemade version (right) are equally effective if used correctly and responsibly. BELOW A throwing stick (depicted here in action) can be surprisingly effective in hunting small animals.

Smooth down the handle to ensure an easy release.

When using the throwing stick, spin it rapidly by flicking your wrist at the end of the throwing stroke, as it will have more chance of hitting the game.

FIRST PRIORITIES

FIRST PRIORITIES

As soon as you are thrust into a survival situation or realize that one is arising, you need to prioritize your needs and actions. One of the first steps is to take firm control of yourself, and possibly of the entire group.

By far the biggest killer in extreme situations is panic, which leads to irrational and ill-considered actions or equally hazardous inactivity. By internalizing the various priorities and options provided here, you will be better equipped to adopt a more rational approach when faced with an emergency.

This chapter deals with key survival priorities – safety, shelter, clothing, water and food – what to take when travelling in different wilderness areas, how to improvise if you don't have all the necessary basics and how best to use whatever you have with you.

You may be faced with a survival situation suddenly, as a result of an accident, or the realization might

grow slowly as conditions deteriorate. Either way, action often needs to be taken as soon as possible. Tempting as it is to rush into a flurry of activity, any action should, however, only be initiated after carefully considering all the options. It would be pointless building an elaborate shelter next to an aeroplane wreck, only to find that there is a danger of fire, or foolish to move without first ensuring that you have taken everything that may come in handy later on.

ABOVE Calming group members and encouraging them to consider the alternatives is a difficult but important role for the group leader when a tense situation or a conflict of ideas arises.
LEFT Rapid attention to an injured group member, without endangering the others, is first priority.

The order in which you try to deal with the main priorities will vary according to circumstances, but in general, personal and group safety should always be high on the list.

Your first priority would probably be to take care of injured or trapped people without, of course, further endangering yourself or the group. Temper heroism with reality. In the case of a vehicle accident, be aware of fire risks or collapsing parts of the structure(s). Salvage what you can safely retrieve from any wreckage, but don't put anyone in danger.

Next, gather the group to ensure that everyone understands the situation, feels involved in subsequent planning and that distraught or anxious individuals are given reassurance. Bear in mind that in the aftermath of an accident, many people may still be in a state of shock. If this is the case, clothing and shelter become important priorities to consider.

Only once your group understands the situation and has absolute clarity on individual roles should you start to look after the basic needs of group members according to the particular survival circumstances in which you find yourselves.

Clothing

With the exception of air and sea disasters, you should have decided what clothing you will need for your trip well in advance. By selecting and packing clothing to accommodate 'worst case scenarios', you will ensure that you can cope and improvise if someone loses their pack and clothing, gets lost without their pack or the group is thrust into an unexpected climatic situation by a disaster.

Cold conditions – either at sea or on land – pose by far the greatest danger. However, extremes of heat and humidity can also create problems to those without appropriate clothing.

Clothing for cold climates

Cold is a killer, and wet and windy conditions can often intensify the effects of low temperatures. Always take enough clothing to cope with unpredictable weather changes, particularly at sea and in high mountain areas. In cold climates, it is wise to follow the principles of layering. Because these multiple clothing layers trap warm air, they provide effective insulation against the cold.

This principle consists of the following layers – firstly a warm, absorbent inner layer of polypropylene or a similar 'wicking' fabric (these fabrics absorb moisture away from the skin) next to the body.

This is then covered by one or more middle layers – these usually comprise a thick cotton, nylon, or preferably fleece shirt and a good-quality down garment, which is very light relative to its insulating value. Other options for the middle layers are polar fleece or similar thick-pile fibres. The final outer layer of clothing should be wind- and waterproof. The best material for the outer layer is a breathable fabric, such as Gore-Tex®, which reduces the build-up of perspiration around your body.

As it becomes warmer, you can avoid overheating by removing the clothing layer by layer. Two pairs of socks (one thin and one thick pair), gloves and a snug balaclava help to protect the extremities from cold and wind. Up to 25 per cent of body heat can be lost via an uncovered head and neck area, and a further 20 per cent through the hands and feet.

LAYERING

| 1. Inner: undergarments, inner boots | 2. Middle: shirt, leggings, outer boots | 3. Outer 1: fleece top, gaiters | 4. Outer 2: cap and windproof layer |

Choices of material

When deciding on the most suitable material, remember that down loses its insulating value when wet, and is difficult to dry out, whereas fleece material retains a good deal of insulation and dries easily. If you are heading for an area which you know will be cold and dry, then down is the best option; if it is cold and wet, your best choice would be garments made from thick fleece.

In the event of an accident or unexpected poor weather you may not even get close to this ideal and you may need to rely heavily on improvisation. Remember that even in temperate areas, persons in shock should always be kept warm.

In all areas, being thoroughly prepared for all the likely weather conditions greatly increases your chances of surviving in comfort.

ABOVE A mummy-style sleeping bag with a good cowl offers effective protection from the cold.

LEFT Items such as seat covers make excellent emergency clothing in a survival situation.

Shelter

The need to shelter from the elements often goes hand in hand with wearing appropriate clothing. Wind, sun and cold all affect the body and you will need to escape or find protection from some or all of these conditions. If you are in a desperate situation and are fortunate, you may have a good tent available, or you may find natural shelters such as caves, overhangs or hollows nearby. If neither is available you will have to create or improvise a temporary shelter. The psychological bonuses of having any form of 'home' should also not be underestimated – a great deal of personal security is linked to having a roof over one's head. As survival focuses so much on one's state of mind, shelter should always be seen as more than merely a physical necessity.

Man-made shelters
Tents

If you have a tent with you, it is possible to camp under quite extreme conditions. By building windbreaks out of rocks, logs or banks of earth or snow and using these to help anchor the tent, you can withstand high winds. Even heavy rain and snow should not be a real problem provided that you dig channels next to the tent to drain the site and clear off the snow before it breaks poles.

Some tents are made of a single breathable material like Gore-Tex®. This material is usually only used in lightweight, high-altitude, extreme mountaineering tents and is very expensive. Most other quality tents usually have an inner, breathable

TIPS ON IMPROVISED EMERGENCY CLOTHING

- Parachutes, sails and even tents (if you have spare or do not need them) can be cut into pieces to make an easy covering. Try to cut large pieces so that these can later be sewn into more user-friendly clothes if the need arises.
- Carpets provide good insulation and warmth, especially for sitting or lying on.
- Seat covers make effective jackets with holes cut in the sides, and can also be used for socks/leggings.

- Thin foam mattresses are useful for body wrapping. If on the move, they can be used as a type of jacket.
- Tents can be used to make temporary shelters and provide warmth when wrapped around someone in shock or suffering from hypothermia. A tent can also be rolled up and used as a covering in windy conditions or in the dark.
- Vegetation such as large leaves makes a handy covering if nothing else is available.

man-made shelters

nylon layer, with a waterproof outer section suspended a small distance above it to allow air to circulate freely and facilitate the removal of body-generated condensation. Ensure that your tent has a built-in ground-sheet of a good quality to prevent any water seeping up from the ground. There are three basic types of tents – geodesic, A-frame and tunnel.

Geodesic: This mathematically designed shape is extremely wind-resistant, and thus highly suited for use in mountains where high winds and snowfall are prevalent. They have the highest strength-to-weight ratio of the tent shapes. Those with three or preferably four poles are more stable than those with only two.

A-frame: This traditional tent shape is also known as a ridge tent. A-frame tents have plenty of headroom and are often less expensive than geodesic tents. However, they are not as stable in windy conditions.

Tunnel: These tents are fairly stable and are generally lighter for their size than geodesic types. Tunnel tents are not as good in heavy snow but they are a good choice in wind.

Ideally, you should pitch your tent away from a steep slope, but not in a basin where you may encounter flooding. If there is a river in the vicinity, check the river flow and be sure not to camp below any possible flood levels. Take note of wind patterns and try to shelter the tent by placing it in the lee of bushes, rocks or trees. When camping in snow, be alert to the possibilities of avalanches and site your tent well away from any potential avalanche zone.

ABOVE A two-pole geodesic-style tent, stripped of its outer shell, is ideal for keeping insects at bay.

LEFT Face the tapered end of a hooped tunnel tent into the prevailing wind to prevent it from becoming dislodged and blowing away.

BELOW The sturdy, inexpensive ridge-style tent is still very popular and used on many expeditions.

Shelter using natural features

If you do happen to get caught out in the open without any form of tent or access to a man-made shelter, the easiest and fastest option is to seek out a natural feature that can be used as makeshift shelter.

Cave or deep overhang: This is a boon if you can find one. Always check for tracks at the entrance to ensure that the cave is not inhabited by an animal you may not wish to meet. Cover the entrance with brush, branches or other material to maintain warmth and shield you from the elements.

Hollows: A hollow or a space under a rock can provide welcome shelter from the wind. Roof it with small branches and any other suitable material you can find.

Logs and fallen trees: A temporary lean-to shelter can be formed relatively easily by scraping out a small depression on the lee side of a log and placing branches or twigs over it.

Under snow-laden trees: Natural depressions form in the snow under the branches of conifers found in forests in the Northern Hemisphere. This space can be enlarged by digging down into snow drifts.

Constructed shelters
Cold conditions

Shelter from the wind is often a high priority in cold conditions. Inside a snow shelter the temperature can remain at a comfortable zero instead of a temperature potentially far lower in the open. Lifesaving options include a trench dug in the snow and roofed by a groundsheet or branches packed with snow, and a snow cave

dug in a bank or glacier. If you need to stay outdoors for longer, construct a good snow shelter.

A trench in the snow can be roofed with blocks of snow and reinforced with branches or other material. This is a useful short-term shelter for one or two people.

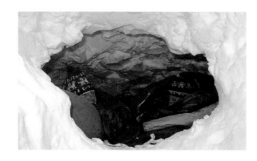

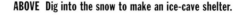

ABOVE Dig into the snow to make an ice-cave shelter.

TOP RIGHT Inuit placing the top keystone in an igloo.

RIGHT Camping under a deep overhanging rock.

BELOW A natural hollow in the rock face can provide excellent protection from wind, ice- or rock falls.

Building an igloo

1. Use a saw or large knife to cut 30 to 40 blocks of snow about 75cm (24in) long, 40cm (18in) high, and 20cm (8in) thick.
2. Stand the blocks on their long edges and form them into a circle, then cut along the top edges to form a gradual ramp. This ramp should rise gradually from ground level to full block height around the entire circumference of the igloo.
3. Place the next layer of blocks onto this spiral ramp, overlapping the vertical grooves of the bottom layer like bricks. Trim the base of these blocks on the inside to give a slight inward lean.
4. Keep adding blocks layer by layer until you have constructed a dome.
5. The roof of the igloo is formed by cutting one last block larger than the hole at the top of the structure and then shaping it to fit. Taper the bottom edges of this block inward to form a 'keystone' that will close tho holo, but not fall in.
6. Make one or more small air holes in the sides of the igloo. Angling them upward from outside to inside will help to prevent wind from blowing into the igloo.
7. Once the structure is built, an entrance tunnel can be dug from outside below the level of the blocks. If properly dug, this tunnel serves as a 'cold air sink'. The cool air gravitates down into this hollow, forming an insulating layer between the cold outside air and the warmer inside air.

Building a quinze

A quinze is a simple form of igloo built from compacted snow.

1. Stack backpacks or suitable equipment to form a pyramidal heap about 1m (3ft) high.
2. Pack snow onto and around this pile of gear. Each 5–10cm (2–4in) layer must be very well compacted by hand, and left to 'freeze' for about 20 minutes.
3. When the structure has formed a dome about 1.5m (4ft) high and 2.5–3m (7–10ft) in diameter, push short sticks if available (if not, improvise) into a depth of about 25cm (10in). This will help you to judge the thickness of the snow when hollowing the quinze out.
4. Dig an entrance and then take out the core of the snow until the packs or gear can be removed. Hollow the quinze out until you touch the bottom of the sticks. Use your hands to compact the snow on the inside.
5. Once inside, use a pack or other suitable item to partially close the entrance and help preserve warmth.

tropical and jungle shelters

Tropical and jungle shelters

In tropical environments, most aspects of shelter construction will rely on improvisation, depending on the circumstances and what materials are available. The useful ideas given here may need to be modified to accommodate a particular situation.

Constructing a tepee: A rough tepee is quick to erect. You will need a few poles of similar length and some form of lashing to tie them together at the top of the tepee. Lash the poles together on the ground, push the rough structure up into the air and spread the poles evenly apart. Digging small holes into the ground to accommodate the pole bases will make the structure more stable.

Cover the tepee with canvas or other suitable material; alternatively, use small branches if nothing else is available. Weave creepers, leaves (palm leaves are ideal) or grass into the covering. You will achieve a much better seal by overlapping leaves thoroughly on top of each other.

Tightly lashed poles of equal length are placed in shallow holes in a circular formation. A fan-shaped covering of hide, canvas or nylon is fastened around the poles at the top, and pegged to the ground with sharpened pieces of wood.

A-frame construction: You can create an effective waterproof A-frame construction by using a canvas sheet, grass or small branches and leaves. In warm regions, bamboo makes excellent building material, but be careful as it can create dangerously sharp splinters when it is cut or split.

BELOW A rough, but readily thatched A-frame hut with side wind shields provides warmth and shelter.

ABOVE Wide-angled tepees offer an increased internal area, but their roofs shed rain and snow less effectively.

Temperate/grassland shelters

Temporary shelters in temperate or grassland areas are essentially similar to those you would construct in a jungle or tropical area. However, providing shade and perhaps protection from marauding animals would be more important than focusing on a rain or windproof shelter

It may be necessary to thatch grass over twigs if you need to make the structure sun- or waterproof. This is a time-consuming process but less elaborate if you simply have to create shade. As with jungle shelters, raise the sleeping platform off the ground if you have enough time and suitable materials available.

Sleeping platforms

Damp ground and crawling insects are part of temperate and tropical forest, and it is always wise to elevate your sleeping platform above the ground. Even for sleeping under the stars, a sleeping platform is a good idea. If you are creating some form of shelter, try to incorporate a raised platform into the design.

After you have constructed the roof of your rough tepee or A-frame, make a sleeping platform inside the structure. Form a frame with four to six upright poles or branches, then lash horizontal support poles across the ends and sides of the frame. Add numerous crosspieces a few spaces apart on which to place your make-shift mattress of leaves and branches or any other suitable material.

It is much easier to incorporate a sleeping platform into an A-frame construction. Simply lash horizontal support poles directly to the frame on at least one side of the shelter and layer with bedding material.

ABOVE This simple sleeping platform shows the cross-piece construction and grass thatching.

desert shelters

Finding shelter in the desert

In desert environments temperature extremes demand shelter – daytime heat and nights that are frequently cold. These both result from the dry air and lack of insulation. Air does not retain heat without a reasonable moisture content, which causes the sun's rays to scorch down during the day, while allowing the daytime heat to rapidly dissipate away at night.

Constructing a shelter from the sun is a priority during the day. It is best achieved by using a sail, groundsheet, piece of cloth or any other available material such as a sleeping bag. The shelter should preferably be lifted off the ground by piling up sticks, stones or your backpack as a base to benefit from the circulating air flow.

The same cloth can also be used to wrap yourself at night to improve insulation. Many desert nomads dig a hole in the sand, and then lay their robes in the hollow. By wrapping in a sail and piling as much sand as possible on top of themselves, they create effective protection against the bitterly cold desert nights.

If you have no form of cover during the daytime, try to locate even the smallest amount of shade cast by rock outcrops or desert plants, however sparse. Covering yourself with desert plants, no matter how dry and scanty they are, will help to some extent. Digging into the sand will cause you to heat up, but if you dig fairly deep, you should be able to reach cooler sand. Climb into the hole and cover yourself with a layer of sand to help shield your exposed skin from harmful ultraviolet (UV) rays.

Vicious sandstorms are common occurences in the desert. If you get caught in one, try to find shelter, sit with your back to the wind and cover your body. By wrapping a cloth loosely around your head, you will still be able to breathe while shielding yourself from the stinging sand that is blowing all around you.

ABOVE An ideal, natural desert shelter affords good shade and allows any breeze to blow through.

TOP RIGHT Use a piece of cloth, a shawl or a shirt to protect your face and neck in a desert sandstorm.

ABOVE Use rocks to weight down sheeting over a natural depression for protection in a mild sandstorm.

BELOW In a severe storm, seek any available shelter, crouch low and cover yourself to protect face and body.

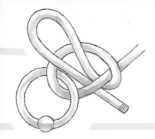
Knots and lashings

Many temporary shelters as well as bridges, flotation devices and other items entail tying poles together. This implies knowledge of knots and some form of rope. It is easy to learn basic rope-tying techniques with some practice; however, rope may not be readily available and you will probably have to devise your own.

How to prevent rope ends from unravelling

Sealing nylon ropes: The end of a rope must be prevented from unravelling. The simplest method of sealing nylon or plastic ropes is to burn the ends. Alternatively, seal the rope by pressing it or rolling the ends with a very hot piece of metal. Make sure that the nylon itself does not catch fire. Do not touch the melted end until it has cooled off – it can impart a nasty burn. You can, however, press and roll the end into a neat finish by wetting your fingers or wearing wet gloves, and manipulating it while it is still hot.

Whipping: This is the process used to prevent the ends of multi-core ropes from unravelling by wrapping them with a thinner rope. Whipping is especially useful for sisal or fibre ropes where the ends cannot be fused with heat.

Good whipping should be tight and neat. Thin cord is far better for whipping than thick cord. This technique can also be used to add grip to axe handles or knives. When having to carry loads or stretchers over a long distance, whipping the handles makes the job much easier for the bearers.

Use a thin cord for whipping and keep it very tight.

Improvised ropes

Unless you are lucky enough to be carrying a good supply of rope, you may well have to create your own cord or adapt whatever is at hand. Vehicles have a variety of material available in the form of electric wire, cord in carpets, seat covers, or nylon bands in some tyres.

In nature, you can use vines, grass, the bark of some trees, leaves and animal hair to make cord of varying strengths. Finer fibres such as those found in aloe stems and leaves, palm tree leaves and willow bark are a good source of thin cord. You may need to plait separate cords together if you need to make a stronger length of rope. Remember to keep the plaits tight when you work with natural fibres. Once you have plaited several lengths, plait three pieces tightly together in order to make a much stronger rope.

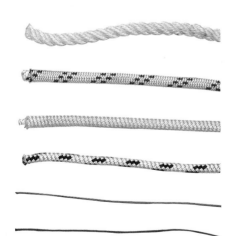

RIGHT A variety of plaited synthetic ropes with varying construction allows for different strengths, (the second from the top being the strongest).

USEFUL KNOTS

There are countless knots with a wide variety of functions. The few basic ones shown here should suffice for most uses in a survival situation. It is vital to use the right knot for the right task – the consequences of a knot coming undone at a crucial moment could be severe.

Reef knot (square knot) with half-hitches

This is one of the most common knots, used to tie two ropes or ends of similar thickness together. It unties fairly easily and is much safer when finished with a half-hitch or even two on each end.

Sheet bend and double sheet bend

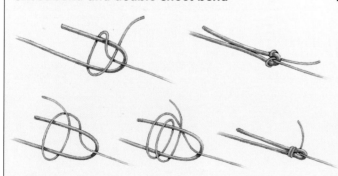

This knot unties easily and is used to tie two rope ends of differing thicknesses together. A double sheet bend is safer, but is more complicated to tie.

Overhand loop

This quick and easy knot holds up well under load and is useful for making nets or joining rope ends. It can be tied in the end or the middle of the rope.

Figure of eight

A much stronger and more effective knot than the overhand loop, it is far less likely to slip and can be tied quickly. This is the usual knot of choice for most climbers when clipping a rope into a carabiner attached to a harness on a climb.

Rewoven figure of eight

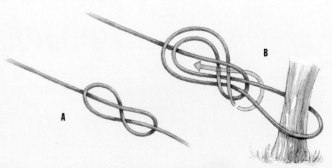

Useful for making a loop around a branch or anchor point. Used by climbers to tie the rope directly onto a climbing harness. It is easy to check whether you have tied the knot correctly by ensuring that the two strands lie parallel all the way, and both exit from the same end.

Round turn and two half-hitches

This easily tied knot is an effective way of securing a line to a post. It can be tied with the rope under a fair amount of tension.

Clove hitch

A valuable knot to start or end lashings as both ends can take strain. The clove hitch can be made in the middle of a rope if you can slip it over the ends of a spar or beam.

Timber hitch

This is used in lashings or to attach a beam or log you want to pull or drag. An extra half-hitch or series of these can be added to assist in holding heavy spars, for example in bridge building.

LASHINGS

Lashing is the term used for tying two or more sticks, poles or spars together using rope. A sound knowledge of lashing is essential to build sturdy structures such as stretchers, bridges, A-frame shelters and rafts.

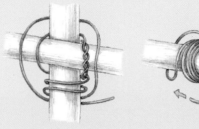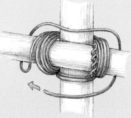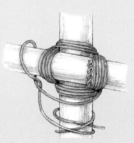

Square lashing *is used to create rafts and stretchers – anything where the poles meet and cross at a right angle.*
1. *Start with a clove hitch or timber hitch underneath the crosspiece.*
2. *Carry the rope over and under spars in one direction as shown, pulling it tight each time.*
3. *Make a full turn around the spar, then wrap in the opposite direction for four turns. Secure with a few half-hitches or a clove hitch.*

Shear lashings *(diagonal lashings) are used to join poles that meet on the diagonal or any form of angle other than a right angle. This is used for making tepees, A-frame bridges or shelters.*
1. *Place a clove hitch on one spar.*
2. *Take a few fairly loose turns around both spars, then loop/tie several frapping (tightening) turns between the spars.*
3. *Finish with a clove hitch around the second spar.*

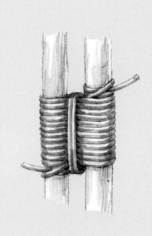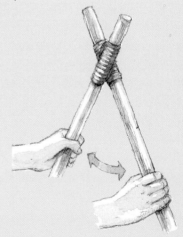

water

Locating water

Water is far more important than food to survive. The body can survive for quite a number of days, even weeks, without food, but for only a few days without water before it begins to deteriorate rapidly and severely.

Human bodies have a water content of about 70 per cent. This constitutes roughly 50 litres (11gal) in a person weighing 70kg (154 lb). Dehydration of up to 5 per cent of body mass can still be tolerated with discomfort, but any more than this and the situation becomes dangerous.

Water intake is controlled by the thirst mechanism. Since the excess cannot be stored in the body after full hydration, it is excreted as urine. Dehydration causes an immediate reduction in the urine output, and increases the concentration of salts and other dissolved waste substances

in the urine. This is what darkens the colour from a normal, clear, light yellow to dark orange-brown. Other very common symptoms of dehydration are dizziness, lethargy and an increasing state of confusion.

Under normal conditions, a moderately active person needs 2–4 litres (4–8pt) of water per day. In true survival conditions you would need more, but you will probably have less than this available. If you find yourself in a situation where it appears that you may run out of water, never assume that rescue will get to you in time – take an inventory of all water and other liquid supplies you have available and enforce a strict regime to conserve and ration them.

Conserving body fluids

The key to maintaining your body's fluid balance is to ensure that the water intake equals that which is excreted. Water is lost through sweat, in urine and faeces, also by vomiting,

ABOVE **The presence of vegetation in the valley indicates a possible source of deep, underground water.**

bleeding and in breathing. Even in very cold conditions, a good deal of water is lost while you are breathing because of the dryness of the air. Restrict your activity to an essential minimum to help preserve your body's water content.

A negative water balance (staying slightly 'thirsty') right from the start will diminish your urine output and aid water retention later, when your body needs it most.

Rainwater

Rainwater is almost universally safe, except after a large volcanic eruption or huge fire (when it might contain dissolved substances or have a high acid content). When it rains, try to collect rainwater by any means possible and store as much as you can in suitable containers.

TIPS ON PREVENTING WATER LOSS

- Try to limit exercise or physical activity.
- In hot areas, rest up in shade during the heat of the day. Even then you are likely to lose 1 litre (2pt) or more per day.
- Eat mostly carbohydrates if possible — these release a little water to the body during metabolism. Avoid dry, salty foods and those high in protein.
- Avoid alcohol and caffeine as they increase urine loss.
- Talk as little as possible, and breathe through the nose, not the mouth.

LOCATING WATER IN DRY CONDITIONS

- Remember that water always runs to the lowest possible point.
- When searching for water, start by trying to reach higher ground or climb a tree to scan the terrain for riverbeds. Water can often be found in seemingly dry riverbeds if one digs deep enough.
- The best areas to start digging for water are those where there is some sign of green vegetation and where the riverbed or stream takes a sharp turn on the outside bank or meets a rock barrier.
- In mountainous areas, search at the base of cliffs or in sheltered crevices.
- On beaches, dig down above the high-water mark and once you hit damp sand, allow time for the water to trickle in. It may be brackish but it is drinkable, particularly once it has been distilled.

Dig for underground water in dry riverbeds.

Water from ice and snow

Ice is easier and quicker to melt than snow. If forced to use snow, then dig down beneath the surface, as deeper layers lower down are more granular and provide denser snow.

Sea ice has a good deal of salt in it, except for older weathered ice (such as icebergs), recognizable by its bluish tinge.

Survivors have found that the best way to obtain water from snow if there is no fuel to melt it, is to form it into compact balls. These should either be exposed to the sun or placed next to one's body in some form of waterproof container. Place the ice balls in black plastic bags if you have them. Remove the ice ball from the plastic and suck water from the bottom of the ice balls.

Water in the jungle and tropics

Most jungles and tropical areas will have rainfall, often on a daily basis. Remember to have containers available to collect any rainfall. Large-leafed plants are a good source of run-off water – tie a few leaves together so that their tips angle downwards into your container.

Palm and banana trees have plenty of water in their trunks. Cut a banana tree off close to the ground and make a hollow bowl in the stump with a sharp object. The hollow will fill with water and although it may take a few hours, it provides clean water that is safe to drink.

To obtain water from bamboo stems, cut a notch at the bottom of a section and let the water drain out. Older bamboo often holds more free water

ABOVE Vines make an excellent water source but avoid those that excrete a milky sap.

than young, green bamboo. Some vines have drinkable water in them – but avoid those with a milky sap, as this is usually poisonous. Note also that certain vines may produce an allergic skin reaction, although their water is perfectly safe to drink.

To obtain water from a vine, cut a notch as high as possible to release the water, then cut the vine low down to allow the water to drain out.

Vines with drinkable water produce copious amounts of free-flowing liquid and are round, not flat. Water from suitable vines will have a neutral or slightly fruity taste and will seem palatable to drink.

Many larger-leafed jungle plants have water trapped in the area where the leaves meet the stem, including some of the large and attractive orchids, as well as bromeliads and pitcher plants. Palm tree stems can contain water that is most easily accessed by cutting the tip off a flowering stalk and bending it down-wards. Coconut milk is safe, but ripe fruits have a strong laxative effect.

Locating water with the help of wild animals and birds

- Follow animal tracks or the flight pattern of birds. Most animals and birds drink in the early morning hours or late in the afternoon.
- Bear in mind that animal tracks can be misleading. As a general rule: if they lead downhill and converge, they could lead to water.
- Birds flying towards water usually approach fast and in a straight line, and in a more meandering pattern away from it. Ducks and geese fly to water in the early morning and away at night. Doves and pigeons usually fly to water in small groups, but return in flocks.
- Larger fish often have accessible water alongside their vertebral column. This fluid can be obtained by carefully gutting the fish and removing the backbone.

Getting water from plants

- Cacti and aloe species are excellent water sources.
- Plant roots often contain stores of water, especially in dry areas. Dig down and cut the root. Then crush it and extract its water by squeezing the pulp through a cloth.
- Dew that condenses on plants, particularly those with broad leaves, can be a valuable water source. You could also try a method used by the Australian Aborigines, who collect moisture from dew by tying bunches of grass to their ankles and then walking through the grass fields.

ABOVE Baboons need to drink daily. By following a troupe, you may be able to locate their water source.
TOP CENTRE Snowgeese head for water in a strict, typical, organized morning formation.
TOP RIGHT On their way back in the evening, they fly in a more random fashion.

ABOVE A barrel cactus contains plenty of water in its stem, but do beware of the nasty thorns.
RIGHT CENTRE The unique shape of the Albany pitcher plant enables it to trap water.

ABOVE Prickly pear fruit is tasty and contains much water. They must be peeled before they can be eaten.

Water purification and filtration

Sadly, most of the world's water has been contaminated by the activities of man – either by heavy metals and other toxins or by human faeces. Some of these substances are impossible to remove by virtually any means – and they can be found in the water of even the most sophisticated large cities. Although they might constitute a long-term health hazard, such traces of heavy metals, organo-phosphates and other chemicals are not of major importance in survival situations. (An exception might be bodies of water such as some wild and isolated high-altitude lakes of the Chilean altiplano, which are heavily loaded with natural and in some cases man-made cyanide salts.)

Human (and in some cases, animal) faeces are a different matter – these harbour micro-organisms such as Giardia as well as other bacteria and viruses that can swiftly lead to health problems. The concept of a 'pristine mountain stream' is almost a modern myth, as even some of the world's most isolated streams carry consider-able debris resulting from careless human toilet habits along their flow.

Despite claims to the contrary, most available portable water filters do not remove all bacteria and microor-ganisms, in particular viruses, let alone chemicals.

Filtered water should be further sterilized by using purification tablets to make it completely safe. If you go from sea level to 4000m (12,500ft) or above, it is wise to treat the water with either chlorine or iodine water purification tablets. Another effective purification alternative is to add five drops of household bleach to a litre of water, then allow it to stand for 45 minutes. The water does tend to have a strange taste, but you can rest assured that it is biologically safe to drink (see purification guide above).

RIGHT Clean sea water can be used to cook food.

WATER PURIFICATION GUIDE

- Select a water supply that is as close to its natural source as possible, e.g. spring or clean snow melt.
- Avoid streams that may have upstream human habitation.
- Gather your snow or ice for melting away from camp sites.
- Always collect drinking water and wash food utensils upstream of a bathing area.
- Ensure that the toilet area is situated well away from water systems.
- Boiling water (just by bringing it to the boil at any altitude) renders it safe for drinking, but uses a lot of fuel.
- Use water purification tablets (iodine and chlorine):
  Follow the manufacturer's instructions and use individually foil-wrapped tablets.
  Iodine tablets are more effective but make the water taste worse.
  Chlorine takes longer and is inactivated by alkaline water.
  Both methods kill viruses and bacteria, but higher concentrations are necessary to destroy Giardia and Amoebae.
  Do not add flavouring powders until after the prescribed sterilization period.
- Portable water filters:
  Effective for removing large parasites such as Giardia and Amoebae.
  They reduce the bacteria and virus con-centration by removing solid material.
  Halogenated filters remove viruses.
  Filtration followed by chlorine/iodine is more effective than either method alone.

- Unproven methods for emergency use:
  Household bleach: five drops added to 1 litre (1½ pints) water.
  Povidine-Iodine (Betadine ®) disinfectant – add a few drops per litre.
  Remove as much water as possible, either by using a cloth filter or allowing it to stand. Then decant the water to reduce the pathogen load.
  Exposing water in a pan or other shallow container to bright sunlight for a few hours will kill most bacteria and viruses.

(Compiled by Dr Lance Michell)

Filtering water

Much of the water you will find will be murky, containing sediment and small pieces of plant and animal matter. The first step in purification is to filter this out by using a good commercial filter if you have one. Alternatively, you can devise your own filter from coffee filter papers, car air filters, handkerchiefs or even old socks.

If all you find is mud instead of water, place it in a piece of cloth, and wring the moisture out into a container. The same applies to any water-containing vegetation – crush the plant in a cloth to extract the liquid.

BELOW Water that is locked into mud or vegetation can be squeezed out and strained in this way. The resulting liquid still needs to be purified.

Commercial water filter

If you dig a water hole in the sand, prevent it from collapsing on itself by lining it with plant material. This has the added advantage of preventing small animals from making use of the water hole. If all other makeshift methods fail and there is no other water supply, filter as much as you can using stone and sand filters, and then drink the water – any diseases can in all likelihood be cured after you have been rescued.

Stills to purify water

A good, efficient still can be used to make sea water and other fluids (e.g. radiator fluid and suspect water collected from various sources) safe to drink. Unless the still is 100 per cent efficient (highly unlikely in field conditions) the water is unlikely to be 'pure', and may still have a strange taste and/or harbour micro-organisms.

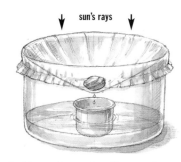

A method to condense and purify sea water.

Passive (solar) still: You will need a container placed inside a larger container or at the base of a hole roughly 40cm (15in) deep and 50cm (20in) across. A piece of plastic needs to cover the large hole. Weight the plastic with a stone or heavy object so it dips towards the small container in the middle. Place the liquid to be distilled in the larger container. It will distil (evaporate) up onto the plastic from where it drips into the smaller container. Vegetation can then be added to produce water by evaporation from the plants.

Solar stills with large diameters are more effective.

Active (steam) still: In the event of a vehicle wreck or breakdown, you might well have the materials to produce a workable steam still. Boil the liquid to be distilled in a semi-sealed container from which a tube (the distillation tube) passes out. Use mud or clay to seal the joints around this tubing. The better the seal on the joints, the less fluid will be wasted.

Cooling water

Sturdy tripod suspends water bucket over fire

Jacket surrounding distillation tube

Distillate

ACTIVE STEAM STILL

the bag, with sticks placed so as to keep the bag from collapsing, or surround the bush with the bag, making sure to seal up all openings. (Pad the top to avoid tearing it.)

• Make sure one part of the bag is placed on a lower level than the rest of the bag (you could dig a small trench) as this is where your water will collect.

A plastic bag makes an effective still.

Transporting water

Transporting water from sources to your camp site or on the move can be a problem. Plastic bags, silvered wine bags or any waterproof container can be invaluable. Look after and try to avoid puncturing them. Gourds can also be made out of some plants such as melons, bamboo and squashes.

By creating some sort of cover (called a jacket) with cooling water running through it (e.g. excess sea water) around the distillation tube, you can distil liquid more efficiently.

Further uses of stills

Most trees and plants transpire ('sweat') a lot of water daily as part of their natural water and food transport system.

• By tying a plastic bag tightly around a branch with a good supply of leaves, you can obtain a fair supply of safe water.

• If you have a large plastic bag and a small bush or supply of freshly cut vegetation you can create a 'bag still'. Place the vegetation in

ABOVE A variety of articles can be used to carry or store water after thorough cleansing. (Clockwise from top): part of an air filter scoop; a hat lined with a plastic bag; a gourd made from a desert melon; a plastic liner in a box.

food from plants

GENERAL PRINCIPLES FOR LOCATING FOOD

- 'All is grist to the mill' (anything that can be turned to profit or advantage) should be the watchword for those in serious survival situations. There is no place for choosiness or sensibilities. The main food sources are plants, insects, larger animals and fish.
- Plants are generally the most abundant and the easiest food to lay your hands on. However, as parts of many plants are poisonous to humans, always take great care. Younger leaves and shoots as well as ripe fruits and seeds are usually safer and more palatable.
- Insects and other invertebrates are a good source of protein. Although the idea of eating insects is regarded by many people as the hardest psychological barrier to overcome, they are quite abundant. Many insects can be eaten raw, although cooking them beforehand may make them more palatable for squeamish individuals who cannot bear the thought of popping a wriggling worm into their mouth.
- Larger animals (birds, buck and reptiles) are often the most difficult to trap or catch, and the hardest for people to kill on sociological and philosophical grounds. Nonetheless, when your survival is at stake you be forced to set aside these concerns.
- Fish are a valuable food source and are often easier to catch than their land-based counterparts. Very few fish have poisonous parts, but avoid the liver of some of the larger game fish and predators such as sharks and barracuda.

Food

We are conditioned to regard food as a daily necessity that is vital and indispensable. This is largely a fallacy, as many cultures who take part in regular fasting and abstinence will testify. Most certainly you need a fair amount of food when exercising, but your body is capable of going without food for long periods of time – far longer than most people realize. In a survival or potential survival situation food should, nonetheless, be rationed very carefully by applying the 'worst case' principle. Some groups experience rather tough times due to unrealistic expectations about being rescued, which causes them to deplete their limited food supplies rapidly, instead of rationing them. It is worth remembering that any plant a monkey (NOT a baboon) eats is usually edible to man. This is not true for other animals and birds – many consume plants or seeds that can be harmful to humans.

ABOVE The fruits eaten by monkeys can be consumed by humans. Getting up into the tree is another matter.

Locating food from plants

Palm trees: A good source of food – the coconuts and other fruits as well as the soft heart of the young stem or branches can all be eaten.

Pine trees: When dug out of the cones, the seeds of this tree form a tasty, nutty food source.
Leaves of a pine tree can also be boiled to provide a type of tea.

Lichens: This safe, non-poisonous food needs to be boiled to soften it. Lichens can also be used to create a watery soup.

ABOVE While lichens are not very palatable, they are edible after they have been cooked.

ABOVE Many parts of wild plants and fruits such as the stems, roots, inner stalks, pips, pods, leaves and seeds provide valuable sources of water, food and medicine.

PLANT TEST

- Do not take chances — if in a group, only one person should test each plant type.
- Test leaves, stems, seeds or fruits and roots or tubers individually.
- Smell: if a plant smells of almonds (hydrocyanic acid) or peaches (prussic acid) when crushed, discard it immediately.
- Skin: rub a piece of crushed plant lightly on a soft skin area (e.g. inside of the arm). Wait at least five minutes to check if any rash, swelling or burning appears.

- Mouth and surrounds: place a small portion on the lips, then the corner of the mouth and the tip of the tongue. Chew a small amount, but don't swallow. Wait at least 10 seconds between each phase. Watch for any numbness, stinging sensation, soreness or burning.
- Swallowing: chew and swallow a small amount, then wait for at least three to four hours before eating anything else.

Perform the same tests for cooked plants, especially the swallowing test. Cooking may alter the chemical substances. If the tests don't cause any adverse reactions, the plant may be considered safe to eat. **DO NOT EAT PLANTS UNTIL YOU HAVE TESTED THEM THOROUGHLY AND ARE SURE THEY ARE SAFE.**

Sea lettuce: Marine algae are usually edible and although there is no truly poisonous seaweed, some can cause stomach irritation. The common sea lettuce and kelp are found along beaches around the world, and both make safe and nutritious meals. They should first be washed, then boiled. Do not discard the leftover water, it makes a nutritious soup.

Nuts and nut-like seeds: These are found on many plants and are an excellent source of much needed protein. Fortunately, very few nuts are poisonous or harmful.

Fern species: Many types of ferns, particularly those found in the Northern Hemisphere, can be eaten. None are poisonous except for mature plants of the bracken fern (*Pteridium aquilinum*), which is the most common species. To be safe, it is better to eat only young ferns – those with tightly coiled fronds. Remove the irritating little hairs that cover many fern species before you eat them.

ABOVE Sea lettuce is nutritious and easy to harvest.

food from animals

Animals as a food source

Many people opt for vegetarianism on religious, philosophical or health grounds. Mankind can survive quite happily on a completely vegetarian diet and in many ways it is the easiest food to obtain. In certain survival situations, however, plants might be difficult or impossible to obtain, and the decision might have to be made – however repugnant it may be to some – to turn to animals as a source of food. Smaller animals (including insects, grubs, marine invertebrates, molluscs and reptiles, as well as fish and birds) are easier to accept as a food source and are often simpler to trap or catch.

A surprising diversity of creatures can form indispensable food sources – the more dire your situation, the more welcome they will be, however unusual they may seem to you.

We are accustomed to buying our meat in aesthetic, neatly packaged form, thereby distancing ourselves

from the real source. No wonder then that it can be difficult for some to accept the reality of stalking, catching and killing a soft-eyed doe, or feeding on the carcass of a beautifully plumaged bird. The harsh reality of survival, however, often demands that civilized niceties be discarded in favour of pure survival ethos.

The aim of this section is not to encourage people in non-survival situations to head for the wild, build traps and snares to catch an animal and then simply cast it aside.

Some snares and traps are down-right nasty and designed to be lethal. It is a good idea, however, to practise making snares and traps. Prior knowledge would be very helpful in a real survival situation. If you do accidentally catch an animal during a practice session, treat it with dignity. Try to avoid injuring it, and release it if you can. If the animal is seriously injured you might have no option but to kill it as humanely as possible.

Remember to dismantle any snare or trap before you leave the area.

Most of this section deals with those animals found on land. Fish and other aquatic creatures as food sources are discussed separately on pp64–71.

TOP A valuable food source, but one that may pose a moral and ethical dilemma for some.

LEFT Locusts are considered delicacies in many parts of the world, but avoid the bright red species.

BELOW Removal of the tail and sting makes scorpions safe to eat. Be careful when you catch them.

Animal patterns

Animals, like humans, are creatures of habit. They follow set patterns of feeding and drinking and many make permanent burrows or homes. The first thing to do in a survival situation when food is becoming a priority is to look for traces left by animals and birds. Take the time to examine paths through the bush – however faint – to establish whether animals regularly move along them. Carefully study the tracks; you may obtain valuable information on the size, numbers and even the type of animal that uses them. It would be far easier to catch an animal on its regular route or trap it in its nest or burrow, than to stalk it in the open. Hibernating animals in colder areas are fairly easy to remove or dig out once you have found their lair.

By spreading your group out along the route and by careful observation you might be able to find an animal's usual resting, feeding or drinking place. This is the ideal spot for an ambush and here you can begin working out how you are going to trap it.

It is pointless trying to trap any of the larger carnivores – their meat is usually rank and difficult to eat and it can easily make you sick. Herbivores such as buck, as well as some smaller carnivores and omnivores (e.g. seals, birds and monkeys) are usually far more suitable prey.

Do not forget the abundance of small reptiles and amphibians – with the exception of warty toads, these are all edible. However, it is wise to remove the skin of these animals as some have glands in the skin that secrete a harmful mucus. Lizards, geckoes and snakes are excellent potential food sources. In the case of snakes, cut the head off well behind the mouth to avoid contact with any poison glands (see bottom diagram).

ABOVE A nourishing snack is often under your nose, such as this rock leguan (iguana) on a locked tent.

ABOVE An armadillo makes an unusual but tasty meal once it has been cooked and removed from its armour.

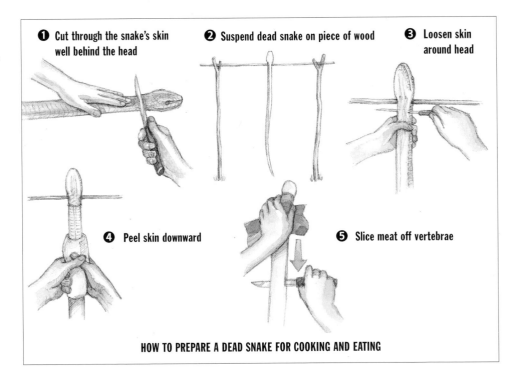

❶ Cut through the snake's skin well behind the head

❷ Suspend dead snake on piece of wood

❸ Loosen skin around head

❹ Peel skin downward

❺ Slice meat off vertebrae

HOW TO PREPARE A DEAD SNAKE FOR COOKING AND EATING

snares

Snares and traps

Snares and traps can be made with various materials and devising your own versions is a key element. Wire, flex, cord or string – if you have them at hand – are invaluable if you wish to construct an effective trap and can also be used to build many different types. If you do not have any of the above available, you will probably need to make deadfall traps, pits, or balance traps.

Trapping and hunting requires energy – you may have to weigh up food gain against the loss of energy and decide when to abandon the hunt in favour of just sitting quietly.

Simple loop snare: This remarkably effective trap can be made from any cord, but wire or a smooth, rigid nylon are best. Create a running loop – twist the wire into a small eye or tie an overhand knot in one end, then feed the free end through it. Tie the free end to an anchor to prevent it from being dragged away. The loop must close easily and the diameter should be appropriate to the size of your prey. Use small twigs to hold the loop open.

Ground-based spring snare: Attach a simple noose to a strong, supple tree or branch. This will cause it to whip up when triggered by the animal, ensuring that the noose tightens fully and holds the animal firmly.

Adjust the height of a simple loop snare to your prey.

Notch a supple, upright branch and drive it firmly into the ground. Then fit a trigger bar into it (see diagram opposite top left). The free end of the snare passes from the trap loop to a firm attachment knot on the trigger bar, then – under tension – to the bent branch. Construction of the trigger

TIPS FOR TRAPPING

- Patience is the key word – remember that animals are wary and shrewd. They do not rush into traps willy-nilly, and have to be coaxed or led into them. You may spend many hours or days before you catch anything. Do not be discouraged – persist.
- The best spots to set traps are where the animal's natural trail passes under a tree or rock, or where it is funnelled into a small opening, perhaps by dead branches or rocks. You can artificially construct such an obstruction, but it may have to be done in sections and left in place for a few days before you set your trap, so that the animal gets used to it.
- Avoid shiny cord or wire for trap construction. You do not wish to alert your prey.

- Try to remove all human scent from the trap and the surrounding area. Animals are extremely sensitive to, and wary of, strange smells. One way of doing this is to wash your hands if you have spare water and then rub them in sand or mud, or in a mixture of sand and the animal's droppings before handling any trap materials.
- You could 'smoke' the trap materials and your hands (or preferably your whole body) over a fire, although this might discourage certain animals such as monkeys from approaching the trap.
- Once you have identified and know your prey, set as many suitable traps of as many different types as you can manage to conceal in the area.

- Get your trap materials set up as much in advance as possible, then cause minimal disruption in and around the area. Spread sand and leaves over any areas you have touched or walked on.
- Trapping close to the nest or burrow can be tricky – animals are at their most cautious close to their home.
- Be aware of prevailing winds; if your scent is carried downwind it could alert the animal at a crucial time.
- Bait the trap with a suitable food to entice the animal but again, try to avoid touching it. The longer you have been out in the wilderness, the less obvious your human scent will be.
- Check traps frequently.

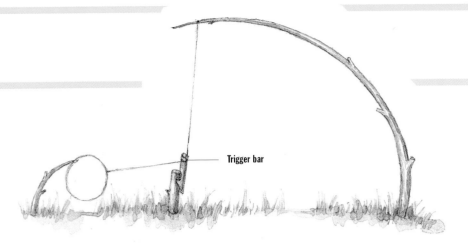

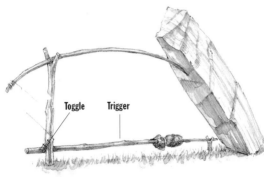

Ground-based spring snare — as with most traps, it is best to conceal the trigger bar and even the bent branch with loose grass or leaves.

bar is vital, and can be refined with practice. Suitable bait can be used to attract the animal. Countless variations exist on the snare shown above. Improvise according to the size of the animal, and the materials that are available.

Deadfall trap: These traps are quite difficult to make, but they are very sensitive, highly effective and definitely worth the effort.

Some can be constructed without cord and are suitable when you have no wire or string available. They can be used for small or large prey (as long as your trap is big enough). When the animal steps in to take the bait, it is crushed by a large weight.

A successful deadfall trap will require a good deal of patience. Experiment until you achieve the right balance and release tension.

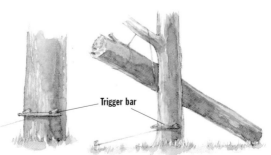

Deadfall log trap showing enlarged trigger bar.

A deadfall rock trap will release its weight when the trigger mechanism is activated.

The simplest deadfall traps use cord or string attached to a trigger bar, which is released by the action of the animal. If you have no such material available, you may have to make your own ropes.

The size and sensitivity of the trigger will depend on the size of your intended prey.

Attaching 'bait' to the string will lure the animal and ensure that it pulls to release the food, thereby releasing the deadfall (a large weight such as a log or rock).

Take great care when setting these traps. Triggers need to be responsive, but a number of hunters have had their creations fall on them instead of the animal for which it was intended.

Spear trap: These traps need cord, which is used to release a toggle (see diagram below). They are very effective for catching wild pigs and buck, but are potentially lethal and should never be set where people may come walking by. Also, remember to disassemble or de-rig spear traps before you leave an area.

Place bait so that the animal is forced past the trigger mechanism (or fasten some bait to the release cord itself) to improve your rate of success.

The shaft is held under tension by a toggle stick with a short cord tied to an upright, such as an adjacent tree. A stiff loop of rope or wire (lock ring) creates tension by means of a short 'floating' stick situated behind the upright anchor. The toggle pulls the lock ring off when triggered, thus releasing the sharp, tensioned spear.

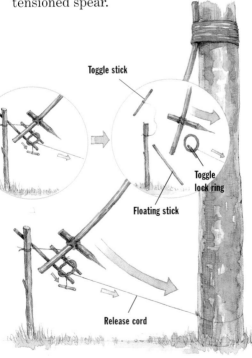

Spear trap with enlarged trigger mechanism (inset).

hunting

- Use tracks and animal spoor to help locate pathways of movement. Follow this downhill to find watering holes.
- Do not move on the pathways if you want to trap or hunt an animal — always keep a distance away or your prey will smell you.
- Choose an appropriate location where you can hide near the track (behind a rock or large trees).
- Animals are very alert at watering holes — rather hunt them on their way to or from the water.

- Hunt at first light if you can, or at night when game is more active.
- Any movements you make should be very slow. Freeze in position if the animal(s) seem to have detected your presence.
- Always keep downwind of the prey (keep the wind in your face). By moving quickly in an uphill direction in hilly country in the early morning, you will prevent your scent being carried upwards by thermal currents. You can then hunt downhill without alarming the animals.

Before lashing this knife in place, some 10cm (4in) of the branch tip was carved flat to help keep it firmly attached. If you only have one knife, beware it does not fall off the spear and get lost.

Tracking and hunting weapons

Tracking and hunting animals is more difficult than snaring, and can demand much energy. Observe some helpful basic principles, and ensure that you have reliable weapons.

Hunting weapons

Catapults are easily made if you have elasticized material (such as an inner tube or even elastic from clothing) and can be very useful in hunting small game and birds. It is possible to become incredibly accurate with only a small amount of practice.

One Himalayan survivor rescued in a dire state of starvation later admitted that, had he only thought of it, he could easily have obtained food from birds in the area.

His pack contained all the materials he needed to be able to build a good, strong catapult.

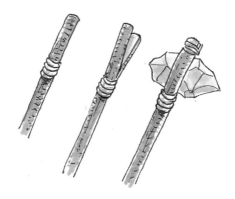

ABOVE A sharpened hard stone lashed into a split green stick makes a useful axe.
BELOW A catapult is handy for hunting birds.

A *spear* is an age-old weapon that can be very effectively used to bring down large prey such as buck and badgers. It can also be used in fishing (see pp64–7) and as a hiking aid. Fastening a knife or sharpened piece of metal to the front makes the spear more efficient. Practise throwing a spear from a crouching position without having to stand up as this alerts animals.

ABOVE Four different types of makeshift harpoons for spearing game or fish (see p66).

HOW TO MAKE A BOW

1. Notch the ends of the supple branch you want to use as a bow with a sharp knife.
2. Fit a loop of tough string to both ends under tension.
3. Lash the loops in place with more cord.
4. Ensure that your arrows are a suitable length.

A traditional weapon

The *bola* is used by South American *gauchos* (cowboys) to trip even large animals, allowing them to get close enough to spear or club them. It is also useful for bringing down birds.

The bola consists of six to 12 long leather thongs (40–100cm; 15–40in) tied together firmly at one end. The other end of each thong is tied around a piece of cloth that holds a golf-ball-sized stone.

The weapon is twirled above the head and released when the correct speed and momentum have built up.

Making arrows

You need straight wood or perhaps even a piece of a spare tent pole or a suitable vehicle part, such as a section of a fuel or brake line. One end needs to be notched to accommodate the string and the other sharpened. Alternatively, it should have some form of point firmly attached to it.

Attach vanes to the end if you have suitable material (e.g. feathers, hard light plastic, tough leaves, cloth or even paper). They will improve the flight of your arrow and can either be lashed in place with cord or stuck on.

A *bow and arrow* is probably the most useful weapon as it can kill at a great distance. It could take a lot of effort to make this weapon but the rewards are considerable.

Making bows

You need a hard, springy wood (e.g. young spruce, cedar or eucalyptus) or a piece of flexible plastic or metal for the bow.

Do not discard car springs, snow skis (if you are sure you have no further use for them) or even metal stays in some backpacks – they can all be used to make a smaller bow.

The ends need to be notched to accommodate the string, which can be any tough, thin cord.

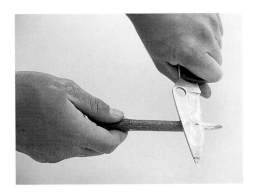

RIGHT Sharpen a straight piece of wood (60cm; 24in long) and notch the other end to make a simple arrow.

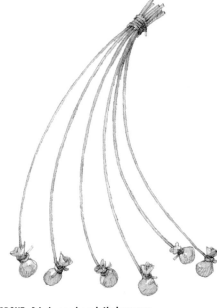

ABOVE A bola can be a lethal weapon.

fishing

FISHING TIPS

- Fish are wary creatures. They can see movements above the water, so avoid casting a shadow on the surface and sit well back from the bank.
- Fishing is generally most successful at night or in the early morning hours.
- Lights (including flaming lamps) often attract fish at night and can be useful when trying to hook or trap them.
- Fish tend to concentrate in calm, deep, shaded pools of water when the weather is hot, and along the edges of sunny patches when it is cool.
- Worms, frogs, crabs and other bait can be found by digging around the edges of a pool or along the riverbank. Once they have been removed from their shells, snails are irresistible to most fish.
- Pre-baiting a likely looking fishing spot by sprinkling bait on the water surface can help to attract fish to the area.
- Live, wriggling bait attracts fish more effectively than dead bait.
- If possible, it is useful to have some form of net or gaff to land the fish you catch, as many are lost at the last moment before they leave the water.

A gaff and net, whether they are commercially manufactured or a rough adaptation, will help to land a fish.

ABOVE Fish will rise to a variety of lures, spinners and bait. Small live insects and invertebrates are good bait.

LEFT Improvised hooks made from a key ring, safety pins, wire, branches and thorns. Create a firm attachment point by notching wood or forming a closed loop in metal. Sharpen the point with a file or on a stone.

Fishing

Fish are a valuable food source and in addition to their high protein content, also often contain large amounts of fat as well as vitamins and minerals. All freshwater fish and most marine fish are edible, although some are more palatable than others.

It is often best to descale and de-bone fish before cooking and eating them although this is not necessary with smaller fish (e.g. sardines and minnows). If the skin of the fish feels slimy, wash the mucus off thoroughly, then rub it with sand to ensure all traces are removed. In some fish the mucus on its skin may be toxic.

Certain common marine catfish have poison sacs attached to large spines on their fins, as does the trigger fish, which has spines sticking out from its belly. Stonefish, scorpion fish and zebra fish – found largely in tropical and subtropical waters – all have similar poisonous spines. Some reef fish, including the porcupine and puffer fish, which both inflate when startled, build up dangerous toxins especially but not exclusively in their livers. Generally, avoid reef fish that have 'parrot-like' beaks or slimy, mucus-covered skins. Fish can inflict painful injuries with their sharp teeth or spines, while electric eels (found in South America) can deliver a powerful shock. Watch for crocodiles in fresh water or sharks in the sea when spear fishing – they may be attracted by the struggling movements and blood from a speared fish.

Useful fishing equipment

Hook and line is the accepted although not necessarily the most effective fishing method. If you have ready-made hooks, you are lucky; if not, you will need to improvise using sharp objects, even thorns and wood. Rods are not essential but are useful to cast over distance, keep shadows off the water and land the fish. A float keeps the hook buoyant and makes it easier to identify a strike.

Lures can be made from brightly coloured materials (feathers, plastic, buttons, cloth or carved wood) and combined with flashy pieces of metal and plastic. The more they resemble 'the real thing' (insects, small fish or worms), the more likely they are to succeed. Lures and spinners are most useful when being trawled by hand or from a boat.

Fish traps

Traps are useful as they can be set and left, with you inspecting them at convenient times and intervals. By damming a stream, you can divert the flow into a net or other trap.

Bottle trap: Cut the neck off a plastic bottle, invert it, then jam it back into the bottle. Insert some bait into the main body of the bottle. Small fish cannot find their way out after having swum into the bottle.

ABOVE The two halves of a large plastic bottle can be used to trap small fish such as minnows.

Twig trap (crayfish trap): A larger and a smaller funnel are created using sticks tied together. The spaces are then either filled in with more sticks or with cord to create a mesh through which the fish being hunted cannot escape. The large funnel is closed at the narrow end.

The smaller funnel, which ends in a narrow open cone, is inserted into the open end of the large one. If you sharpen the tips of the smaller funnel it helps to prevent fish from return-ing through this constriction once they have swum in.

LEFT AND RIGHT A funnel trap consists of two parts: a small inner funnel that fits into a larger outer section. The inner funnel is fitted with sharpened spikes, which allow fish in, but not out. Cord is used to create an escape-proof mesh.

Sock trap: Place bait inside a sock, then, using a loop of wire or a plastic ring to hold it open, place the sock in a stream. Eels, in particular, can be caught in this way. The smellier the bait, the better, so animal entrails (and even dung) can be used as bait.

ABOVE A makeshift trap made of a sock or pillow slip can be used to trap smaller fish. The trap is held open by using a ring made of wire, or the neck of a plastic bottle as depicted above.

fishing methods

Other methods

Harpoons: These can be useful for catching large fish that come to the surface or when spearfishing from the bank or in the water. Tridents or multi-point harpoons increase your chances of spearing and holding the fish. You must strike fast, and it often helps to start with the barbs already submersed. As water refracts (bends) light, you may need some practice before you succeed. If looking down into the water, aim for a spot below the position you see the fish.

Running lines: You are more likely to catch a fish by suspending a series of hooks on lines in a stream or dragging them behind a boat. Placing the hooks at different depths ensures that you cover all levels of fish activity (see diagram below).

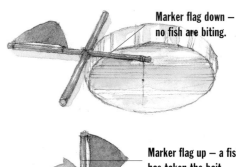

Ice hole with fishing sticks: Fishing in very cold areas where the water surface has frozen will entail cutting or knocking a hole through the ice (see above). Be careful that the ice beneath you does not break. Ice fishing is like any other method – it is best to set up many lines and to try different depths and types of bait. A useful accessory is a marker flag joined onto a crosspiece that will jerk erect if a fish is hooked (see diagram right). The faster you get to your catch once alerted, the more likely you are of hauling it in before it becomes a meal for a hungry seal or other predator.

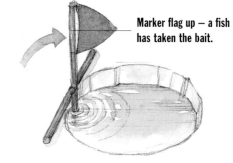

Marker flag down – no fish are biting.

Marker flag up – a fish has taken the bait.

TOP AND ABOVE Ice-hole fishing.

Sea fishing

Fishing from a boat has distinct advantages when the craft is moving because fish will be attracted by any spinners that turn and flash in the water. Numerous hooks can be placed on one long line, which can be dropped astern. Many fish are also attracted to the shade of the boat and will swim around it for hours. Turtles, which make an excellent meal, also seem to be attracted to boats.

A net with the right-sized mesh for the size fish you are trying to catch can be used to form a 'fish pool' on the

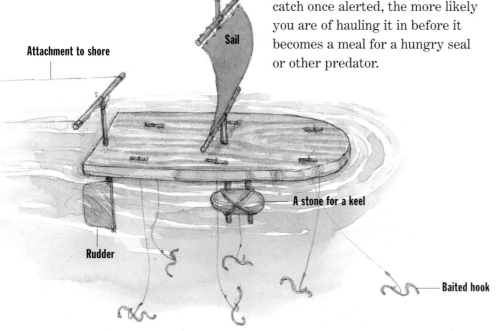

Attachment to shore

Sail

A stone for a keel

Rudder

Baited hook

A small 'boat' can be used to carry baited fishing line out into deeper water if you cannot reach.

water surface or catch fish at depth. By closing the net rapidly around a school of fish, you may be able to trap quite a substantial amount at once.

A good net size for medium-sized (0.5kg/1lb) fish is to make the mesh large enough so that it just fits around an average adult wrist.

Constructing a net

Nets have many uses – for catching fish, collecting food and for making hammocks – and can be made using any twine or cord. Cord should ideally not be too thin; parachute cord is a good option or even insulated electric wire (although this tends to slip if it is not tied very tightly).

The easiest net to make is a tie-off net (see diagram right), in which cow (girth) hitches (see top of diagram) are used to attach lengths of cord – drop threads – to a top rope suspended between two posts or trees.

The net is started with strong cord for the top and finished with the same cord at the bottom (leave enough to tie off the net ends to prevent slippage). If you have only thin cord available, double it or plait several strands together.

Adjacent drop threads are then tied together sequentially, using overhand knots (see bottom of diagram). The net is finished by tying the double drop threads to the bottom rope with a clove hitch, or a round turn and two half-hitches (see p49).

Use a pre-cut piece of plastic or wood as gauge to ensure mesh of uniform size. Additional rope will be needed to tie your net to support logs, floats or weights.

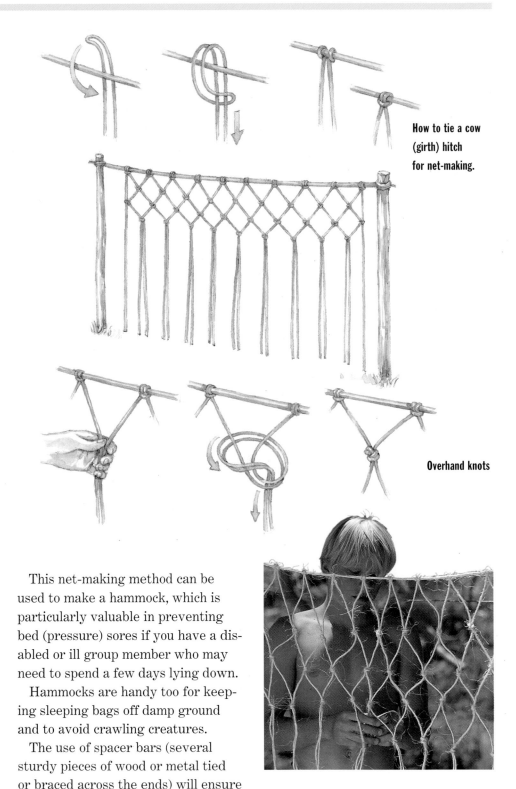

How to tie a cow (girth) hitch for net-making.

Overhand knots

This net-making method can be used to make a hammock, which is particularly valuable in preventing bed (pressure) sores if you have a disabled or ill group member who may need to spend a few days lying down.

Hammocks are handy too for keeping sleeping bags off damp ground and to avoid crawling creatures.

The use of spacer bars (several sturdy pieces of wood or metal tied or braced across the ends) will ensure that the hammock still remains firm when you lie back in it and does not fold around you.

ABOVE A tie-off net can be made with any length of thinnish cord or twine. The mesh size is determined by the size of the intended prey.

food preparation

Food preparation and preservation

Most food needs some preparation to make it more palatable or to remove poisonous or harmful sections. In the case of animals, skin, fur, feathers, scales and bones often need to be removed. Larger animals are best skinned hanging up, preferably from the head as this makes it easier to remove the internal organs. A good skinning knife has a sharp blade, but a rounded end – this enables one to separate the skin from the underlying tissues without cutting it. Once the separation has started, skin can often be peeled off by hand.

In a true survival situation, you would eat parts of animals that would usually be thrown away. In fact, very little cannot be eaten.

ABOVE A camp fire – heat for cooking and comfort.

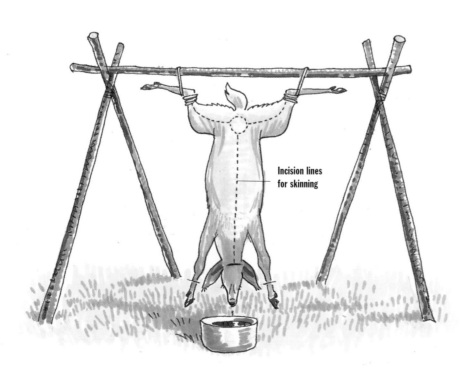

Incision lines for skinning

Before being skinned, venison must be hung to drain the blood from the carcass. The blood should be collected in a bucket or pot as it provides valuable nutrients, but must be used quickly as it does not keep fresh for long.

Cooking food is an accepted part of our lives – in many cases, food does not actually need cooking and the process actually destroys many vital nutrients such as vitamin C. It can, however, make certain foods more palatable by softening meat and vegetable fibres. Also important is the fact that hot food is generally a great morale booster.

Other advantages of thorough cooking are that it can destroy harmful bacteria and parasites, and neutralizes poisonous substances in some plants (such as old potatoes, nettles and leeks).

Circumstances might force you to eat food raw – do this with the knowledge that cooking is a luxury that has only recently (on the broad evolutionary scale, anyway) entered into man's diet plan, and our bodies are actually biologically adapted to a diet of primarily raw foodstuffs.

FOOD PREPARATION TIPS

- Meat and fish can be preserved by various methods i.e. boiling, smoking or drying (in desert or cold latitudes).
- Offal (lungs, liver, intestines, heart, kidneys etc.) is not easy to preserve. These should be eaten first, even though this might seem the wrong sort of order of events. Although lungs have little nutritional value they can be used as bait.
- Cut meat to be smoked or sun-dried into very thin strips, remove the fat, and then string or spear it onto sticks or racks.
- When smoking meat, one of the simplest ways of making a 'smokehouse' is to close off the sides of a tripod stand made over an open fire.
- Remember that the smoking process requires lots of smoke and a slow-burning low fire. Avoid wood with a lot of resin or a very strong smell, as this may make the meat inedible.
- It can take many hours (or days) to smoke meat thoroughly to ensure that it is dry but still retains a small amount of moisture.
- Sun-drying needs time and can only be attempted in warm, dry climates. If you have salt available, rub this into the meat to aid preservation. However, bear in mind that this could make you more thirsty later.
- Watch for flies —they could lay maggots in the meat.

RIGHT A drying rack for fish or meat strips will ensure that the process does not take too long and spoil your store. A small fire in the middle will allow you to smoke your supply.

Preserving and transporting food

If you need to move from a location where you have built up a store of food, you will need to take supplies with you. Methods discussed here of pickling and smoking food will help ensure that it is preserved. Salt is a good preservative, but should be washed or wiped off the foodstuffs before you use them, particularly if you have insufficient water supplies.

ABOVE Lemons, limes or similar, with salt if available, make good pickling fluids that help to preserve vital foods. In general, the stronger the solution, the better the preservation.

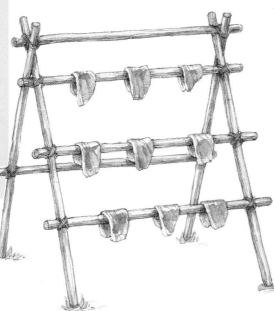

To prevent food from spoiling, it must be dried completely, or be preserved in pickling liquid.

Large gourds as well as thick pieces of bamboo can serve as carrying containers if you do not have any purpose-built ones. Ensure that they are dry before you use them.

Seal openings with beeswax or a plastic bag. Clay can also be used, but it cracks easily when it gets dry and could contaminate the food in the container. Mix thin pieces of bark or grass into the clay to bind it.

If you have dried or smoked meat, wrap it in large leaves, but open and check for mould regularly.

Other preservation methods

The acids of limes and lemons (citric acid) are useful to pickle fish, meat, and even vegetables. Use a lot of juice with equal parts of water.

A very strong salt solution can also be used to pickle foods. When a raw potato, tuber, egg or onion begins to float in a salt solution, it indicates that the brine is strong enough to use as a preservative.

Fruits and some vegetables can be preserved by cutting them into thin slices before they are sun-dried or even smoked. Lichens and seaweed can also be dried by using these methods after they have been boiled. Once they are completely dry, grind them to a powder which can be used to add flavouring to soups and stews.

Nuts and grain cereals easily turn mouldy. Smoke or sun dry them (or dry them directly on hot rocks) before storing them, preferably in a sealed watertight container.

food from invertebrates

Food from invertebrates

The best and easiest protein and general food sources often go unnoticed for a long time in survival situations simply because the survivors are not attuned to eating them.

Invertebrates – the so-called 'lower life forms' – are abundant in most parts of the world and have value as a nutritional food source. Strange comfort may be gathered from the virtual certainty that you have probably already eaten a number – albeit unwittingly – in your food.

ABOVE Termites are plentiful and nutritious.

TIPS FOR COLLECTING AND USE

- When collecting insects and other small invertebrates, be on the lookout for spiders, scorpions and centipedes, many of which can give you a nasty (or even fatal) bite or sting. Spiders and centipedes should generally be avoided as a food source, although scorpions can be eaten once their tail (and hence the sting) has been removed.
- Brightly coloured invertebrates, including snails, are often poisonous and best avoided.
- Certain cone-shell snails, found in the tropics, can inject a small dart, which has been known to cause serious nerve damage and even death. Avoid these conids.
- Hornets, wasps and bees can provide a good meal. Nests contain larvae and pupae — tasty, nutritious food — and of course bees make honey. Balance the dangers of being seriously stung against the value of a food source. Smoke can make bees drowsy, kill them, or drive them off the nest, but if there's not enough smoke it can also drive them into a frenzy and they will attack mercilessly. Any member of your party allergic to bee stings must be very cautious.
- When dealing with bees, cover your entire body and head with thick, sting-proof clothing, or swaddle a sleeping bag or similar around yourself. Bees are inactive at night so this is the best time to try to extract honey from a hive with the aid of copious smoke.
- Most small invertebrates can be eaten raw and offer better food value when uncooked. To make them more palatable, they can be boiled, roasted on hot stones or directly on a fire. Remove stings, wings, legs, hairs on caterpillars (which can be singed off in a flame), and the hard outer casings of beetles or larvae.
- Worms, slugs and grubs have superb food value. When air-dried or smoked, they often look far more appealing. Slugs can be roasted and snails boiled or fried.
- Insects, particularly small ones, can be dried and crushed to form a paste. This can be used as an additive to soups and stews. Locusts and grasshoppers are common in all countries — they are deservedly regarded as a delicacy by many African tribes.
- Termites are an excellent food source. Their large mounds, which can be broken open to yield both mature adults and grubs, are easily spotted. After heavy rains, termites perform mating flights and can be easily gathered in large quantities. They can be eaten raw, roasted or fried. Dried and ground they make a very nutritious and easily transportable food supplement.
- A simple pit trap consisting of a container (e.g. a cup) in a hole, with a log or stone to cover it, can be effective in catching insects. Placing sweetened water, honey, fruit or other sweet substance in the container will act as an additional attraction.

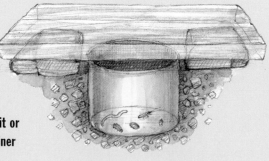

A simple insect pit trap

Marine invertebrates

Nearly every coastline offers a rich harvest of food. Virtually all shelled creatures can be eaten, as can most types of marine invertebrates. If you are fortunate enough to be marooned at the seaside, food is unlikely to be a major concern.

ABOVE In need, even this small crab will make a welcome meal for a hungry survivor. Where there is one, there are many more — be on the lookout for small breathing holes in the sand, which often indicate the presence of sea slugs or sand mussels.

ABOVE A migratory bee swarm such as this is not a good source of food as it will take a number of weeks before a new hive, full of honey, has been established.

BELOW Grubs tunnel inside dead or decaying trees. When fried they taste like roasted peanuts.

TIPS ON CATCHING MARINE CREATURES

- You can usually find shellfish by digging down into the sand close to the tide line as they often come closer to the surface at night. A distinctive V-shape as the water runs back in the shallows (below) signals their presence. Shellfish can move back down their burrows rapidly, so dig quickly while flicking the wet sand aside.

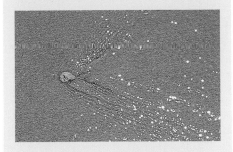

- Salt, vinegar or even lemon juice can provoke shellfish and burrowing worms and prawns to come to the surface.
- As filter feeders, shellfish can build up dangerous quantities of pollutants (such as lead and mercury salts) as well as the red-tide diatoms. Be aware of this. Shellfish should be boiled and eaten soon after harvesting. Leftovers are best discarded.
- Crabs and crayfish (lobsters) must be thoroughly cleaned. Always remove the gills and stomach before eating. Remember that the claws contain good amounts of meat.
- Red bait can be collected from the rocks at low tide. The inside can be eaten, as can the insides of sea urchins and starfish.
- Avoid jellyfish, sea anemones, coral and similar marine animals. They have little nutritional value and their stinging cells can contain poisons.

FIREMAKING TIPS

- Ensure that there is adequate ventilation – fires produce a lot of harmful gases, and also consume oxygen.
- If building a fire in the midst of vegetation, clear an area of at least 2m (6ft) around the fire – more if there is a strong wind, and if the surrounding vegetation is particularly dry.
- Take care not to make the fire too close to overhanging branches.
- Always make sure that the embers have died down completely before leaving the area. This is especially true of deep embers that may smoulder for days.
- Build an earth bank or a circle of stones around the fire to contain it, or dig a trench around it.
- For wet or snow-covered ground, light the fire on a platform of green logs or place it on a detached part of a vehicle.

Fires and firemaking

A fire for warmth, light and cooking is arguably one of the most valuable things in the wilderness. It offers comfort and can make a tremendous difference to a group's physical and mental wellbeing. In a survival situation, fire can often spell the difference between life and death.

Making a fire is simple if you have a cigarette lighter or matches. Waterproof matches (see pp25, 27) are still the best.

If you are fortunate to have some method of making a fire, be careful to preserve it and thus your store of matches. Once you have used them all, lighting a fire will become very difficult, if not entirely impossible.

Having to make a fire with minimal materials under difficult conditions such as high wind, cold or rain is an art that deserves some practice. You should not leave this to chance – imagine using your last match and then accidentally smothering the fire because you were too hasty in adding more fuel.

Of all disaster scenarios, fires pose the greatest threat to both man and animal. A fire that is allowed to get out of control can turn into a runaway conflagration with horrifying speed and demolish a forest and everything in it in a relatively short period of time. Be very careful where and how you make a fire.

Tinder: This is needed to start a fire. Any dry, fine, combustible material such as paper, moss, tree bark, dry leaves, grass, animal dung or fungi will allow a spark to take. It may be necessary to crush or grind the material first to make it fine enough to flare easily.

Kindling: Small leaves, sticks and pieces of dry bark form the next additive to the fire once the kindling has caught. Add these slowly and carefully until a clear flame is visible.

Main fuel: Fuel should always be added progressively to avoid smothering the fire. Small sticks need to go on first, then large branches or logs as the fire takes. Greenish wood or wet fuel can be dried out next to a fire to provide the next load of fuel.

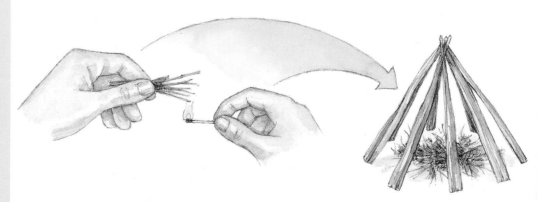

A bunch of dry tinder is used to start a pyramid fire.

ABOVE Dry grass, twigs and branches with a dash of petrol are quick fire starters.
TOP RIGHT A magnesium block.

Alternative fuels

Many substances will burn, particularly fuels, plastic, rubber and cloth. Some of these, particularly plastics, give off noxious gases. Use them only as a last resort and ensure the fire is lit in a well-ventilated area.

Oil and petrol can be persuaded to burn more slowly by pouring them into a container of sand and lighting them. Oils and diesel fuel burn more readily when mixed with petrol. Hydraulic fluid and pure anti-freeze are also flammable.

A useful way of getting a 'lazy' fire to start is by flaming it with an aerosol can. Many aerosol propellants and contents burn well. However, be careful – if used for too long the nozzle can get hot enough to melt.

Lighting a fire without matches or lighters

You may have no conventional firelighters. There are numerous other options, although none are quite as easy as they sound. A really worthwhile exercise is attempting some or all of these when you are not in a survival situation – it will have the combined effect of making it easier to use them in dire need, and of persuading you to carry emergency matches in every pocket and container you can.

Strong sunlight, focused through a magnifying glass or even fairly strong glasses, can start a fire. Binocular and camera lenses generally have so many elements that the heat is lost internally, but they can provide a number of useful lenses if broken open.

Flintstones generate sparks when they are struck against one another, or with a hard piece of steel. Sparks should be directed into a bed of very fine, dry tinder. Magnesium blocks are highly inflammable and are found at outdoor stores. The scrapings from these blocks provide superb tinder.

A car or other large battery (even lamp batteries) can produce sufficient sparks to light a fire. Beware, as this depletes a battery and can cause it to heat up. If you are using a car battery, remove it from the vehicle first.

A little petrol poured on a cloth lights very easily. Be sure not to use too much, and stand well back when igniting the cloth. Gunpowder, too, can be used to light tinder. It must never be used by children and should only be used if there is no alternative.

ABOVE Hitting a machete against a rock will create sparks to light a fire, but may also ruin the blade. Note the pile of fine, dry tinder at the base of the rock. As soon as smoke appears, fan it by blowing into it gently.

Carefully break open the bullet and pour a little gunpowder on the tinder, leaving the remainder in the bullet (wedged in lightly with paper or cloth). Place the bullet in the breach and fire your gun directly next to the tinder. The gunpowder will ignite and the now-smouldering cloth or paper can be placed on the tinder.

You are unlikely to have chemicals available, but your survival kit may contain potassium permanganate. You should also have sugar, while glycerine is found in many first-aid kits. Mix the sugar and potassium permaganate (one part sugar to eight or nine parts of potassium permanganate), then add the hand-warmed glycerine. It should flare up after a while. You may even be able to ignite this mixture without glycerine, by grinding it between two rocks.

Different styles of fire

Apart from the normal pyramid fire (see p72), you can build fires that make more efficient use of available fuel, and are less hazardous.
Star fires take their name from the circular arrangement of logs (big ones work best) that point to a central fire. The logs are pushed inward as more fuel is needed. Rocks can be placed in the spaces between the logs to provide cooking platforms and to hold the logs in place. One or more reflector shields will help you to direct warmth to you or the group.

NOTE: Rocks may split or crack in fire, particularly wet or porous ones. Beware of flying pieces of rock: they can cause serious injury.

ABOVE AND BELOW The heat of this trench fire is contained by the trench sides, and the effect of wind is reduced. The sand dug out can be used to cover surrounding grass, avoiding the danger of the fire spreading.

A *trench or pit fire* is placed in a hole to shelter it from strong wind. This reduces the danger of flying sparks. As this method diminishes ventilation to the fire it is best to place a layer of fairly large rocks on the bottom and build the fire on top of them.

A *tin, or 'hobo', fire* uses a good-sized tin, with a few holes knocked in at the bottom and around the lower side to form a very fuel-efficient stove. It is best to cut a panel at the base that can be folded back to regulate air supply and allow for the insertion of fuel. Various options exist for the top – one entails punching holes in the top to allow anything placed on it

A flat-top 'hobo' tin fire elevated for ventilation.

to cook slowly. You can also cut a single large hole to accommodate your pot, and place the fire on stable stones for improved air circulation.

Preparing hot meals

Cooked foods are more palatable, and the heat will eliminate potentially harmful bacteria and parasites. Warmth obtained from hot food can make a critical difference to body temperature in very cold conditions.

Under normal conditions, outdoor cooking can be an art and a pleasure;

under extreme circumstances, it may become a desperate and onerous duty, albeit an essential one.

If you have a stove, metal cooking pot, and a range of utensils, your task is simplified. If not, you will have to devise makeshift pots and pans from tin cans, hubcaps, parts of vehicles, gourds and bamboo; as well as carved wooden spoons, twig forks and a branch pot holder. A surprising amount of cooking can be done without using any conventional utensils.

A simple spit is useful for suspending cooking pots, as well as whole carcasses, and for drying clothes. Using heavily branched sticks for the upright allows you to adjust the height of the spit by moving it up or down onto the branch stumps.

A cantilever pot holder (see below left) allows the pot to be swung off the fire for stirring or inspection. The support stick has to be very stable.

Many things can be cooked directly on hot rocks. These can either be heated up in a fire and removed when needed, or the fire can be made on a bed of rocks. When the fire has burnt out, the rocks can be swept clean, and the food cooked on top of them.

Use a tray to catch the fat dripping off a spit roast.

A cantilever-style pot holder needs a strong branch.

Once the fire has died, the rocks will retain heat and can be used as a stove to slow-cook food.

stoves

If you have no container at all, you can wrap food in a suitably large, non-poisonous leaf (for edibility test, see p57). Then plaster the leaf with mud and place this 'mud sandwich' on a bed of coals, layering more coals on top if possible. This method is a slow but effective way of cooking most meals.

If you are going to be at a site for longer, it is worth the effort to build a Yukon oven (see below).

First hollow out a pit with an extra channel on one side that will allow you to add fuel. Build a fire in the pit, arrange stones around it in a circle and pack them with clay, adding further layers of rock to form a 'chimney'. The top of the chimney is used as a cooking hole and platform. You can add fuel to the fire from the hole left at the side.

A deserted termite mound can be used as a chimney, and the base then hollowed out as a place for the fire.

Variations of the above include the insertion of a metal box to make an oven in which you can even bake bread. Any size or type of metal box with a lid can be built into the side of the Yukon oven to make it more versatile and even more effective.

Cooking with camping stoves

If you are venturing into wilderness areas in foreign countries where mini gas cylinders or specialized fuels may not be readily available (such as large parts of Africa and South America), you would be advised to take a *multi fuel stove*, which runs on petrol, benzene, paraffin and even raw alcohol.

Multifuel stoves tend to be noisy and difficult to light; they are also subject to fits of temper (flare-ups, blocked jets), but are efficient and allow users to burn a variety or even a mixture of fuel. It is wise not to use

BELOW Cooking with gas inside a tent can be dangerous as the pressurized gas canisters are sometimes unreliable, especially after frequent use.

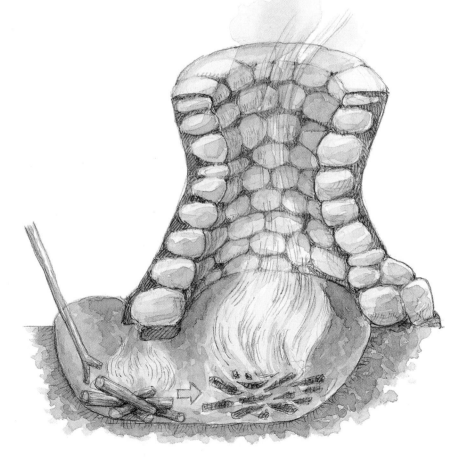

ABOVE The Yukon oven uses the convection principle.

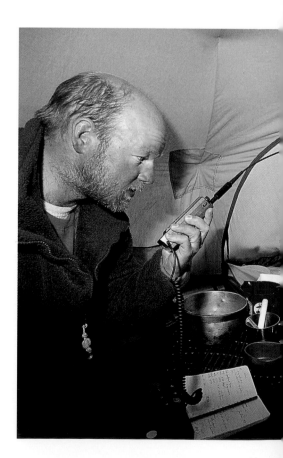

ABOVE A pot on the boil is always a welcome sight to weary ice climbers as warm food and drink raises the core temperature and helps prevent cold injuries.

these stoves in tents or other confined spaces as the pressurizing system is not always completely reliable, especially after periods of heavy use.

Most multifuel stoves work well at altitude, but their temperament counts against them at extreme altitude, where a user's thought process may be sluggish and unreliable.

Meths stoves use methylated spirits or ethanol (known as 'cooking alcohol' in many parts of the world). Most of the available models come as compact fold-up units, complete with kettle, pots and windscreen.

Standard camping gas stoves are the best for lightweight camping trips as they are small, compact and easy to use. They do not burn well at altitude on their normal butane fuel, but have been used with special propane-butane mixes, right up to the highest camps on Mount Everest. They light easily with a controllable flame. Cartridges must be empty before they are removed (never throw them into a fire as they can explode). Do not change cylinders in the vicinity of open flames.

ABOVE A hanging stove is useful in stormy conditions as it prevents the food from spilling.

RIGHT An aluminium set comprising gas burner and stove with a flask for decanting warm fluids is a 'must-have' on a hiking trip.

Gas stoves with removable cartridges can be stored and carried separately from the cartridge, which can also be used on a matching gas lamp when it is not needed for the stove. The propane-butane fuel mixture is readily available, and produces more heat. Many fuels found in fuel bottles are poisonous, and all are highly inflammable. The best containers are aluminium bottles which are light yet strong, with screw-on lids fitted with appropriate rubber or plastic washers. Ensure that fuel bottles are distinctively marked to avoid confusing them with water bottles. If possible, you should use a permanent marker to label them correctly (add a warning symbol). Alternatively, paste a clearly written label on the container and cover it with transparent plastic.

MOVEMENT

MOVEMENT

The choice between moving or staying put is sometimes a difficult one.

Of all the actions taken in a disaster situation, this requires the most careful analysis.

Both courses of action may have advantages and disadvantages; both may encompass elements of risk.

People who find themselves in a predicament are generally tempted to 'do something', to rush off and look for rescue, or find their own way out of the circumstances. Before embarking on any course of action, sit down and take careful stock of your predicament. Immediately after your situation has arisen, you and the members of your group may still be in a state of shock, and decisions taken hastily or at an early stage may not necessarily be the best ones. Movement should be seen as the last resort unless there is a clear-cut route to help and rescue or rescuers are unlikely to find you easily in your present location.

RIGHT A breakdown with a lone vehicle in wild country means walking out or waiting for help to arrive.

Preparing to move

If moving seems inevitable, then make sure that the group is as well equipped as possible and that you have taken everything that might be of use. This applies particularly

to any items that may be useful in erecting quick forms of shelter. If you are abandoning a vehicle, first ensure that all possible items of survival value have been taken.

Depending on the terrain, it may be easier to carry supplies or move injured people by creating a sledge or some form of backpack. The simplest option is to tie clothes or cloth into a sausage-shaped pack or a pouch that can also be useful if you need to move small children.

Ensure that all group members know the intended route in case someone gets lost.

Before moving on, remember to leave some clear form of message for rescuers, indicating your direction of travel and time of departure, particularly if you are abandoning a vehicle.

Navigation using maps

If in unknown territory, finding your way is best achieved with a map and a compass or GPS, which should be in your kit. Maps are useful as they indicate the following:

- *Direction* via north–south lines (or grid lines) on the map. Once a map is orientated, then natural features on the map such as rivers, hills and valleys should match what you see on the ground.
- *Distance* via the scale of the map. Maps have different scales and thus varying degrees of accuracy. A hiking map usually has a scale from 1 : 25,000 to 1 : 50,000 (e.g. at a scale of 1 : 50,000, for every cm you measure on the map, there are 50,000cm in reality on the ground). This means that 1cm on a map represents 500m; 1in represents 50,000in. Detailed hiking maps of, e.g. 1 : 10,000 (1cm = 100m or 0.4in = 328ft) show more features but cover a more restricted area. Aeronautical charts are usually 1 : 250,000 and give you a good idea of surrounding areas, but don't provide too much detail.
- *Heights* are given via contour lines, which also give an indication of the slope or gradient and spot heights (e.g. peak heights of 4500m or 14,765ft). The contour interval is the vertical height difference represented by each line, usually about 10–20m (40–80ft). The closer together the contour lines, the steeper the slope. Take careful note of slope angles. A cliff or steep drop-off is indicated by many contour lines that virtually meet.
- *Special features and geographical landmarks* i.e. lakes, rivers, cliffs, roads, buildings and vegetation.

CHECKLIST – MOVING VS. STAYING

The following checklist will help you consider some or all of the potential factors before you take your final decision on whether to move or not:

- What type of situation are you in? If a vehicle is involved (e.g. a car, ship or aeroplane) it might be far easier for searchers to spot it than a group or individual on foot.
- Is anyone likely to know your present location? Are you still on your scheduled route or have you moved far off the original route plan? Do you know where you are relative to your original route, or to a road, railway or some form of civilization? If you left the area, would you simply be heading off blindly in an unknown direction?
- How well do you know your location? If you don't know the area, can you establish whether the nature of the terrain is suitable to the skills of the group? Are the potential hazards such that movement is an unwise option?
- If there are injured group members, how serious are their injuries? How easily can they be moved? Should victims be moved at all?
- What is your food, water and equipment stock? How long do you estimate your current provisions will last?
- How long do you think it would take before someone realizes you are missing and reacts accordingly? What is your estimated time of arrival and by how long has it been exceeded?
- What are your chances of being found or rescued? Do you have a realistic idea of how long it would take to be found if someone did launch a rescue operation?
- Do you or your group have any special needs? Do any of your group members need special medication (e.g. for chronic conditions such as diabetes or hypertension)?
- Is splitting the group a viable option? Would it be feasible to send some members for help and leave the rest of the group behind?

ADVANTAGES OF STAYING PUT

- *Movement requires more energy – conserving energy allows your food supplies to last longer.*
- *It provides the opportunity to make a more permanent shelter.*
- *The risks are known – hiking off into unfamiliar terrain may expose you to greater hazards.*
- *You can plan and implement some signals to alert rescuers, such as burning tyres to make smoke.*
- *Injured, old or sick members of the group will not be exposed to the stress or rigours of a move.*

ADVANTAGES OF MOVING

- *It might be psychologically better for the group to take action than to 'hope for the best' and wait things out.*
- *Good shelter, food and water might be easier to obtain elsewhere.*
- *If rescue is unlikely for some time and resources are insufficient, then movement can save the day.*
- *If camp is made in one area for an extended period, hygiene might deteriorate, making sanitary conditions more hazardous.*
- *If at high altitude, it might be necessary to descend to maintain the health of the group.*

using maps and compasses

Orientating your map

A map is only really of value if you can match it to your present position and the surrounding terrain. This will give you a better idea of where you are and the direction you need to take when moving. The first objective is thus to orientate your map to the terrain and to north.

Orientation via terrain

If you know exactly or even roughly where you are and visibility is good, then you can often line up your map with the help of prominent features such as hills, peaks, rivers or lakes. Study the map carefully, then turn it until the features shown by contours and other means match the terrain you are in.

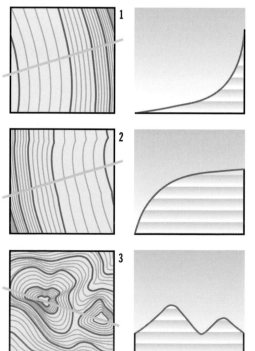

RELIEF MAP SECTIONS
1. A concave slope. 2. A convex slope. 3. Two summits

Orientation via compass

The easiest way to line up a map is by using a compass or some other method of finding north. It is advisable to do this anyway, since lining up the map via the terrain could be completely inaccurate. The most suitable compass for walking and map-reading is the Silva type, which is fairly inexpensive, robust, and easy to use.

Magnetic north and true north

The map must be lined up with north: remember that maps show true north on their N–S lines. This differs from magnetic north (shown by the compass) by a varying number of degrees according to where you are on the earth. (The magnetic north pole is not exactly at the earth's geographical, or true north pole). This difference is known as magnetic variation (or magnetic declination).

The map should have a legend giving magnetic north as: e.g. 'magnetic variation (or 'declination') 15 degrees east'. This means that the magnetic pole actually lies 15 degrees east (rightwards) of true north in the area covered by that map, so the compass reading is 'inaccurate' by 15 degrees east (right) of true north.

Rotate the map 15 degrees westwards (left, or anti-clockwise) from the compass north (magnetic north) to line up on true north, so it matches up exactly with the terrain as you see it (see diagram A).

Many maps have three arrows to show different variations: magnetic north, true north and grid north.

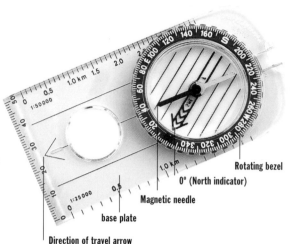

Rotating bezel
0° (North indicator)
Magnetic needle
base plate
Direction of travel arrow

The Silva-type compass is an excellent navigational tool as the rotating bezel allows bearings to be set with ease and the useful direction-of-travel arrow makes it simple to follow a bearing. Beware of metal objects (e.g. a vehicle) deflecting the compass needle.

The latter system is favoured by the military and by some countries including England and several Western European countries. However, the difference between grid and true north is so small as to be insignificant for any non-military purposes, so grid north lines can be taken as true north.

Using the map only

Once the map is orientated, you can use it to establish your exact position. You are then able to plot your most suitable pathway e.g. 'down the valley on our east, over the neck, down the southwards ridge to the road'. Simply follow your selected route using the features shown on the map to guide you, while continuing to keep a careful eye on where you are on the map by matching the features surrounding you on the ground.

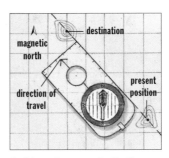

A. Orientating a map destination

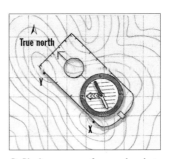

B. Placing compass for map bearings

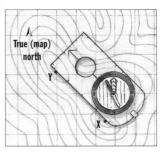

C. Orientating a bezel to true north

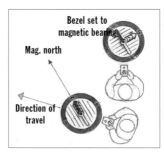

D. Turn body with the compass in your hands until the needle lines up with north on the bezel

Using map and compass to navigate

At night or in poor weather conditions you may have to depend on a combination of the map and the compass to move. The compass bearing will thus show you which way to travel. Bearings run from 0° (north) via 90° (east) through 180° (south) and 270° (west) with the full circle being at 360° (north again).

- You must first know precisely where you are on the map – your present position (see diagram A).
- Then choose your destination on the map.
- Place the compass (see diagram B) so that the edge of the base plate (i.e. the direction of the travel arrow) runs from your present position (x) to your destination (y).
- Rotate bezel so that the north mark on the bezel lines up with the north–south lines (pointing to true north) on the map (diagram C).
- Read the figures where the direction of travel arrow meets the bezel. This is known as your true bearing (diagram C).
- Convert this to magnetic (compass) bearing by adding or subtracting (as given on the map). If the variation is given as '12° west' then add this to the magnetic bearing. If it is given as '12° east', then subtract it from the magnetic bearing.

In this particular example, if you were in Africa and the map declination was given as 12° west, and you had a map (true) bearing of 280°, you would then add the 12° declination to give your final 292° magnetic (compass) bearing.

- Set this last bearing by placing 292° (on the bezel) opposite the direction of the travel arrow on the compass.
- Hold the compass level so that the needle swings freely.
- Rotate until the needle's north end (red) lines up with the north arrow on the bezel.
- The direction of travel arrow now shows the way you must head (see diagram D).

In brief, the north needle of the compass always points to magnetic north, and you have just set on your compass the direction (i.e. at the direction-of-travel arrow) in which you must go.

Providing you keep the compass' north needle lined up with the north arrow on the bezel and follow the direction of travel arrow, you will be heading towards your destination. In this specific example, 292° is virtually northwest.

Also use other clues (i.e. the sun and the stars) to check that you are moving in the right direction. Guard against orientating the map to south instead of north (this will result in you being 180° off course) or using the wrong end of the compass needle.

It is easy to 'feel that you are going the wrong way', particularly at night or in mist. However, trust the compass and keep checking that you are moving according to the direction of the travel arrow. If you have done everything correctly, then your compass will be pointing the right way.

FINDING DIRECTION WITHOUT A COMPASS
If you have a compass or can improvise one, then locating north is fairly easy, but bear in mind that magnetic deviation may vary in different world regions. If not, there are several ways of finding direction by using natural features.

The sun

The sun rises roughly in the east and sets roughly in the west. There is quite a bit of seasonal variation due to the tilt of the earth on its axis. If you are in the Northern Hemisphere, the sun is due south when at its highest point in the sky. The opposite concept will thus hold true for the Southern Hemisphere.

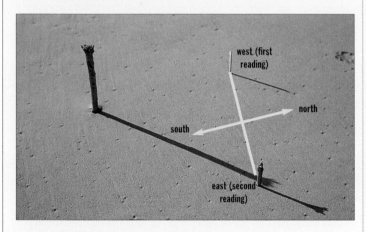

*A **Shadow Stick** can be used to find both your direction and the time of day.*
Locate an east–west line by using a long vertical stick to mark off the trace of the shadow.

Mark the point at the tip of the shadow (this will be marked W), then wait at least 15 minutes before you make another mark on the shadow tip (marked E).

Join the two marks to get the east–west line. (Note that north–south will be at right angles to this.)

The longer the time interval, the more accurate the line will be.

Remember that the shadow moves clockwise in the Northern Hemisphere and anti-clockwise in the Southern Hemisphere. The diagram above shows a Northern Hemisphere reading.

The stars

Stars appear to 'move' across the sky because of the rotation of the earth. As the north, or pole, star is at the axis of rotation, it 'stands still', and can thus be used to find north in the Northern Hemisphere. If location is a problem, then use the distinctive Big Dipper and the position of the Milky Way to identify the pole star.

It helps to get your bearings by finding south. When you have found the conspicuous Southern Cross and its two pointers, use an imaginary line to extend the long axis of the cross. Next take a line that bisects the pointers and extend it. Where these two imaginary lines meet is the Celestial South Pole. Drop a line straight down to the horizon to give true south.

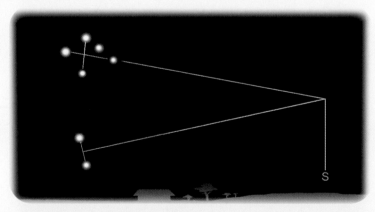

ABOVE Southern Cross **BELOW** North star

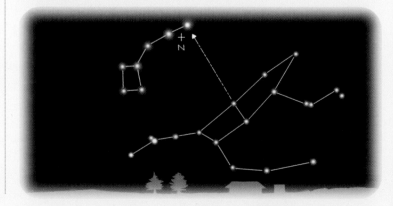

Plants and natural features

If it is cloudy or heavily overcast, various other natural features can be useful in confirming your sun sighting or star sighting at night.

- *River flow:* *If you know the principal direction in which a major river flows in the area in which you find yourself, this would help to confirm direction. Remember, however, that many rivers meander a good deal.*
- *Lichens and moss:* *These grow in greatest profusion on the shaded side of trees – in the Southern Hemisphere this would be the south side, while it would be the north side in the Northern hemisphere (picture above).*
- *Trees and flowers:* *In older trees, the annual growth rings (which can be seen on a tree stump) are larger on the side that faces the Equator.*
- *Flowers:* *These plants mostly face the main course of the sun to flower better – this would be north for the Southern Hemisphere and vice versa.*

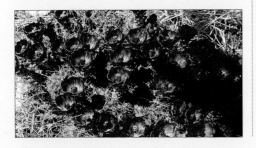

Birds and insects

The African Weaver bird, which is found predominantly south of the Equator, builds its nest on the west side of trees.

The large nests of African Weaver birds give a good indication of which direction you would find west.

In many regions, termites build their characteristic mound nests orientated north to south in order to maximize shade in the heat of day.

ABOVE The long axis of a termite mound usually lies on a north–south line.
LEFT Flowers that face the sun can provide valuable directional clues.

Improvised compass

If you need a compass to navigate but do not have one, you might be able to create a compass needle from a sliver of iron or steel, or a razor blade using one of several methods.

A reasonably strong battery (such as one used for a car or a series of lamp cells that have been connected up) can give a strong enough current to magnetize steel. The harder the metal (e.g. a tempered steel needle) and the tighter the coil, the longer the magnetism will last. Make and break contact quite a few times to fortify the magnetism.

By repeatedly stroking a needle in one direction on silk (or even certain synthetic fabrics), it will become magnetized. Remagnetize regularly as the magnetism in your makeshift compass needle diminishes with time.

If you have a magnet, you can use it directly as a north indicator, or if it is too large for this purpose, use it to magnetize a smaller piece of metal. Magnets can be sourced from parts of many car generators and alternators as well as in some radio loudspeakers and toy motors.

After you have magnetized the metal it must be allowed to swing freely. This is done by either floating it on water or suspending it from a very light thread.

As the needle indicates only a north–south line and there is no indication on which is north and which is south, use other methods (see p82) to decide which end of your improvised compass needle points north.

GPS devices

Global positioning systems and altimeters

Modern tools such as wrist compasses and altimeters (sophisticated watches that also indicate direction, air pressure and altitude above sea level, see below) as well as Global Positioning System (GPS) devices can be extremely valuable in locating position and movement. The GPS system uses over two dozen permanently positioned satellites in the earth's orbit to establish the location of your portable GPS receiver via the triangulation of up-and-down radio signals. The coordinates of your position (where you are on the surface of the earth in terms of latitude – east and west – and longitude – north and south) will appear on the GPS as a set of six to twelve figures known as the grid reference. For example, '1655E2235N' means that your position is 16° and 55 minutes east, and 22° and 35 minutes north. This can help to locate your exact position on a map and may also be used to send positional information to rescuers via radio or cellular phone.

Some GPS devices also give altitude, barometric trends (for weather prediction), plot the course you have been moving or perform the same direction-of-travel functions

as a compass. Perhaps their biggest limitation is that of battery power – be conservative in your use of such devices, because when they run out, they are of no further use.

On the move

Having knowledge of your present position and the terrain will play an important role in determining the level of certainty regarding your movements in a survival situation. Having a map, knowing your location and where you would find some civilization would be the ideal if you find yourself in this situation.

If you have no clue about your whereabouts (following an aeroplane crash or if you get lost in a storm), then the best option is often to follow a watercourse. Most rivers eventually lead to lakes or the sea and are

The triangulation of radio signals activated by satellite is valuable as it can instantaneously establish the precise location of the GPS device in three dimensions – giving latitude, longtitude and altitude. It also tracks any changes in position, thus allowing survivors who may have to move to update their location to search teams.

likely to have settlements nearby. In steep terrain, the river might cut through gorges or meander. Try to follow the general direction of the river according to the lie of the land. When the river widens it can offer a transport mode on a raft.

RIGHT The capabilities of a satellite navigation (GPS) device – held by this traveller wearing a mask to protect his face against a blizzard – are put to good use in a featureless snow-filled landscape.

Group movement patterns

In most cases, it is best to keep a group together when moving. This can be difficult when there are large discrepancies in age or fitness or when there are injured members. The problem of moving is made even more difficult in fog, falling snow, rain or mist, or when moving at night. It calls for organization and discipline, which are not always easy to impose in a survival situation. Most people are amenable to reason, so the most sensible option is to fully explain the additional problems and wastage of time that would result if the group had to search for members who have split up or gone missing.

The best movement pattern for a group is to have a scout (or two, if the group has enough members). The scout should go slightly ahead of the other members to find the most suitable path. Most of the members should follow him or her with the leader in the group, and a responsible person should be enlisted as the 'tail-end-Charlie' to ensure that no stragglers fall behind.

The scouts should not lose visual or auditory touch with the group, and each group member should be made responsible for keeping in constant contact with the person immediately behind and in front of him/her.

It is the leader's responsibility to stop for regular checks and head counts. Every member should know what action to take in the event of being separated from the group. In general, this would entail stopping and waiting for a period of about 30 minutes while calling occasionally.

It is the leader's responsibility to keep members of a group together and moving in an efficient formation so that individuals do not lag too far behind.

Thereafter, if a lost person is certain of the direction from which he/she has come, the most sensible strategy would be to retrace his/her steps slowly, stopping regularly to call and listen for responses.

This situation makes you realize the value of having a whistle in your kit. If each group member includes this item, it greatly improves the chances of locating someone who is lost or missing since the piercing sound of a whistle always carries far further than that of a voice.

Similarly, if every group member knows the intended route and the final destination, it may help them better orientate themselves if they are separated from the group.

There is an exception to the rule of splitting a group – when a small group of physically fit members who are able to move quickly, forms part of a larger, slower group. In this situation, the small group can act as a

scouting party and also focus on finding food, water and shelter or cutting a path for the slower group. However, it is essential to mark the route well to ensure that the slower group are able to find the trail easily (see p89).

Moving over difficult ground

When travelling over difficult or more challenging terrain, it is in the group's best interests to assist weak and struggling members or help one another. On very steep slopes, joining hands can be helpful to anyone who slips or does not feel sure-footed.

Downhill movement can be difficult as your visibility is restricted and it is not always possible to judge the size of drop-offs (cliffs or sudden steep slopes). Decreased visibility is problematic when travelling at night, so move cautiously. You can sustain painful injuries (i.e. a twisted ankle) on downhill sections, which can cause long delays in the group's progress.

Facilitating movement

'Short roping', a useful technique commonly used by mountain guides, may be an option for people who find it difficult to move over downhill terrain. With this technique, a strong, fit member uses a 'tether' or leash to support a less able person. The guide holds the rope tightly to provide support when the person being held needs it. The guide remains above and slightly to one side of the person if possible. With some practice, short roping can greatly speed up group movement while providing support to people who would otherwise feel uneasy on difficult terrain.

If the rope is quite long, the guide can coil the excess around his body and use it to assist someone up or down larger drops.

In the 'short roping' technique, a stronger member holds someone on a tight rein – by varying the slack slightly, he gives the less sure-footed member valuable support on steep, broken ground.

Commercial backpacks

There is a huge variety of commercial backpacks on the market. Most good ones have a well-padded hip belt and broad, comfortable shoulder straps. Internal frames make the pack lighter and more streamlined than the older models. Side and top pouches make it possible to pack frequently used items and emergency gear (i.e. first-aid kits) where they are easily accessible.

No matter how well made, back-packs are seldom truly waterproof. If you are in an area where there is the likelihood of rain or your pack stands the chance of falling in the water, then it is best to wrap everything in several strong plastic bags. These bags have many other uses in normal camping and emergencies and are thus never a waste.

Makeshift backpacks

If you don't have a commercially made pack you will have to create your own. By lashing branches together you can make a pack to tie on your back. This will free your hands for scrambling, pushing vegetation aside, carrying a stretcher or sled, and helping others. Wrap the gear into a groundsheet or

ABOVE A smallish pack is suitable for women or children on weekend hikes as its padded hip belt and shoulder straps ensure comfortable carrying.

LEFT This compact day pack is best for carrying the essentials on a short hike. The hip belt is only slightly padded and offers little support for the load.

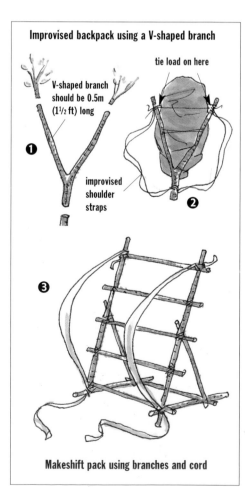

Improvised backpack using a V-shaped branch

tie load on here

V-shaped branch should be 0.5m (1½ ft) long

❶

improvised shoulder straps

❷

❸

Makeshift pack using branches and cord

large piece of clothing and tie it to the frame. Wrap any spare material around the frame to pad it and avoid bruising your back and hips. The broader you can make the shoulder straps of your pack, the better. Again, improvisation is the key.

The *Hudson Bay Pack* (see illustration below) is another handy way of slinging goods across your back and entails tying gear into an oilskin or similar piece of cloth (preferably waterproof). Tie fist-sized stones or similar objects into the diagonally opposite corners of a square cloth (about 1 x 1m, or 3 x 3ft) with strong cord or bark.

Roll your goods in the cloth, then tie the cloth up and lay the bundle across your back or fasten it around your waist.

Route markers
Routes can be marked by cutting marks into trees, tying knots in grass, placing sticks or stones in patterns on the ground or tying pieces of material to prominent natural features i.e. large rocks or trees.

Remember that what you might think is an obvious marker might not be so clear to those who are following, especially if they are tired and sick, or it is raining or snowing. Move back and then up to your marker(s) to check whether they are clearly visible.

Creating sleds and carrying frames
If your move is expected to last long or entail a reasonable distance, or if you have injured people or many bulky supplies to haul, then it would be useful to have a carrying frame or sledge. Depending on the nature of the terrain and the materials at hand, you can either create a two-toed drag sled or a sleigh-type sledge. If the terrain is very rough and hilly and you anticipate the going will be difficult, you may need to create a stretcher for an incapacitated group member and some type of pack for carrying supplies.

Two-toed sled (travois): This is the easiest and most basic sled to create. Any two fairly long branches or even pack frames joined together will be suitable. The sled needs two runners that simply drag on the ground. Join the two runners by using items of clothing (i.e. put the runners through the sleeves of shirts or jackets) or lash on additional smaller branches. One or more people can pick up the rear when crossing rough terrain.

Modified version of Hudson Bay Pack.

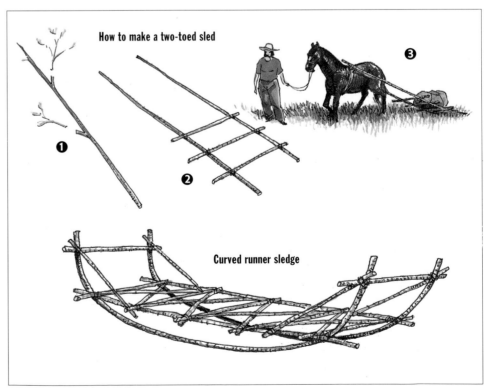

How to make a two-toed sled

Curved runner sledge

The disadvantage is that the dragging toes of the sled can cut deeply into the substrate, making it quite cumbersome to pull. If moving across snow, making small flat runners will improve the sled's mobility.

Curved runner sledge: While this is a slightly more sophisticated version and takes more time and effort to make, a curved runner sledge is much easier to move than the simple sled. It is far superior on snow, ice or smooth ground and can be be dragged on long lines if necessary. Create a suitable curve to the sledge by pulling up the two main runners and bracing them with sticks or cord pulled from the tips towards the back (see diagram p89). If travelling down a steep incline, use a rope if you have one to brake the sledge from the back.

An easy method of transporting a person or goods on snow or sand is to drag them in a groundsheet with padding placed beneath an injured person to make it more comfortable.

Movement at night

Movement at night has many additional hazards and should only be undertaken if there is good and sound reason for it. There are situations where it is unavoidable – in the case of medical emergencies, in desert areas where it is inadvisable to travel during the day and perhaps on snow or glaciers, which become safer when they harden at night.

The main problem in travelling at night is to stay orientated as it is very easy to lose your direction without clear landmarks. On a clear, starry night the stars can be a useful aid but it is difficult to keep them in sight and still keep moving. Other disadvantages of night travel include the inability to anticipate obstacles and steep drop-offs and the usual difficulties inherent in ensuring the group does not split up.

If there are no effective lamps or ones with limited battery power, sit and wait a while before starting out, as one's night vision takes over half an hour to develop fully.

Bear in mind that this important adaptation of your eyes can be destroyed in an instant by lamplight or any other bright light – even a flaring match.

If you need to use a light to read a map or resolve some urgent problem, assign this task to only one member of the group. This will be useful in helping to keep the night vision of most of your members intact.

Other ways of preserving night vision

- Use a red filter over a lamp when map reading. If this is not available, you will be able to preserve 50 per cent of your night vision by using only one eye when the light is on and keeping the other tightly shut.
- Try to focus slightly to one side of the object you are viewing – the rods (the eye's vision cells that see in black and white and are best for night vision) are located off-centre.
- Another useful tip to preserve night vision is to slowly scan your eyes in a circular fashion to get a better night image of an object.

Triplet method of route retention – Phase 1 establishes the line.

Phase 2 shows people leapfrogging the line.

Route retention

Maintaining your line of movement at night can be very difficult if there are no visible landmarks. One way of keeping your line is to use the slow but certain 'Triplet method (see diagrams p90). Once the direction of the march has been chosen, the 'leader' sets a second person off (the 'aimer'), stopping him/her at a reasonable distance along the line of march. The 'target' person is then sent past the aimer until he reaches the limits of the leader's range of vision, and the leader positions him in line with the aimer. The leader moves up to the aimer, the target person becomes the new aimer, and the original aimer moves up as the new target.

In bad mist or difficult conditions – particularly if a leader has no compass – four people can be leapfrogged to keep a more certain line of march.

River crossing and flotation

Rivers can constitute a major barrier for a person or group, especially if they are tired, cold and disorientated. It is all too easy to underestimate the power of a river and find yourself in serious trouble. Apart from causing death or injuries, getting wet unnecessarily can result in hypothermia (see p114). After any river crossing, try to get group members as warm and dry as possible and be alert for symptoms of hypothermia.

It is often wisest to wait it out if the river seems to be flowing quickly but is likely to subside, or to look for an alternative route. If there is no option, then plan your crossing carefully. Spend some time moving up and

down the bank, studying the river and its flow patterns, and then choose the best crossing point. If you have a sturdy rope then the crossing can be made much more safely.

Ropeless river crossings

Your best method of crossing without using a rope will depend on the width, depth and power of the river and the group's strengths and weaknesses.

For wide, slower rivers it may be best to build a raft or flotation device if materials are available, particularly if there are very old, very young or injured members. If it is only possible to build a rudimentary raft, then use it to tow the weakest members across the water.

You will usually need dry clothes after a river crossing to avoid hypothermia. Before crossing, remove at least long trousers and jackets – if not most of your clothes. Hold them above your head or wrap them in waterproof material or a container.

ABOVE Linking hands is effective provided the river crossing is not too hazardous.

Shoes should ideally be kept dry; wear them only if the riverbed is rocky or there are hidden obstructions underwater. If you only have one pair of socks, wear shoes without them.

Rope-assisted crossings

When using ropes to cross a river, the safest method is a continuous loop. This is only suitable when at least three or more people are crossing. Tie the rope around the waist of the strongest person in the group (helper 1), which is held upstream by helper 2. Another person (helper 3) holds the rope downstream as an emergency measure to help pull the individual crossing back to the bank if he/she experiences problems. By gripping the rope in their hands instead of around their body, helpers 1 and 2 can prevent being swept away by a powerful stream or undercurrent.

river crossings

On reaching the other side, helper 1 positions himself downstream of helper 2 who follows, while being belayed (holding climber safely with a rope) by the other two. Finally, helper 3 crosses with the assistance of the others.

Helpers should never try to pull a person who is swept away while crossing back upstream, as he/she could be drowned by the strong force of the water. It is better to pendulum the person back to the downstream bank by allowing him/her to be naturally swept sideways on the tensioned rope by the water.

If a large group needs to cross a river, the continuous rope loop can be kept running until the last member is safely across. A safety line can also be tied across the river and the group can cross holding on to it while being belayed by another rope. Bear in mind that the tensioned line should preferably be angled downstream.

TIPS ON ROPELESS RIVER CROSSINGS

- Choose a crossing spot with no visible hazards immediately below it and don't cross just above cataracts and waterfalls, to prevent being swept into fast-flowing, turbulent water.
- Cross diagonally with the current rather than trying to fight it. Always face upstream during crossings so that you can see ahead and therefore avoid any debris sweeping towards you.
- If possible, avoid crossing on river bends since water always runs fastest on the outside of bends.
- Take note that rocks and submerged obstacles often cause surface waves. Large boulders in fast-moving water can form dangerous 'eddies' (when a current reverses behind an obstacle) and whirlpools in the river below them.

- Sticks or poles can be used to provide mutual support or hold a group together. If the current is strong, hold the sticks firmly with arms crossed at chest level.
- Crossing in a group line with a sturdy stick or pole for support gives support to smaller, weaker or less sure-footed individuals. The simplest method is to form a line with the strongest person upstream to break the flow of current.
- Another method is to form a group 'huddle' by all facing inwards, linking arms across each other's shoulders and then crossing the river by shuffling sideways. The person on the leading side of the huddle could use a stick for balance as well as to assess the depth and obstacle risk on the riverbed.
- For an individual crossing or wading across wide shallow streams that flow slowly, it is best to use a pole or stick both for support and to test the depth ahead. Hold the pole firmly with both hands.
- If crossing with a heavy backpack, loosen the hip belt of the pack. If you lose your balance you can easily remove the backpack to avoid being swept along face-down underneath it.
- Flotation aids can be made from a waterproofed pack, airfilled long trousers (see p144) or even empty water bottles.
  A tent flysheet stuffed with grass or light but bulky substances (e.g. polystyrene, empty plastic bottles and foam mattresses) may also help with flotation.

LEFT A sturdy log can be a useful support for unsteady members who need to cross a strong flowing river.

building bridges

This makes crossing a the river easier because one struggles less against the flow of the water.

Makeshift bridges

One of the easiest and safest ways of crossing a deep gorge or a narrow, fast-flowing stream is to build a bridge. This is particularly useful if you need to cross a stream regularly, either in a long-term survival situation of a few days or more, or if you need to regularly cross streams around a base camp. The effort of making a log bridge is worthwhile if you can avoid unnecessary falls or sustaining injuries resulting from a slip on wet or icy rocks.

Simple log bridge: The advantage of a log bridge for narrow streams and ravines is that it can initially be built entirely from one side of a river.

The first log (which can be a temporary 'thin' log to save weight) is dug in or braced against other logs close to the bank. It is then raised alongside the bank via two or three ropes until it can be swung and dropped over the gap. Take care that no one is attached to the ropes or is standing inside them – if they lose control, they could be pulled into the gap along with the log. The remaining logs are slid along the first log and manoeuvred until three or four logs broach the stream. Use wooden or metal stakes to peg the logs firmly on both sides. If the bridge is going to be used regularly, consider placing a wood or rope handrail on either side.

HOW TO BUILD A SIMPLE LOG BRIDGE
1. Lower the log. Wrap ropes around some adjacent trees to add more friction if necessary.
2. Then slide the next log carefully across the first one.
3. Remember to peg all the logs down securely before using the bridge.

Sticks help to maintain balance on this short but tricky river crossing.

❶

❷

❸

ABOVE Bamboo poles lashed tightly together with rope serve as an effective and sturdy walking surface in this monkey bridge.

ABOVE Side ropes can help to improve the stability of longer swing bridges.

the bridge if necessary by pulling on the ropes that anchor the X-frames. The bridge can be made more stable if you place tensioned ropes out at roughly a 45° angle back from the top of each arm of the X-frames.

Trestle bridges: Building a trestle bridge properly is time consuming but it might be the best option if a heavy load (i.e. a stretcher or even a vehicle) needs to be transported across a gorge. The link between the transoms can be made from logs or even several ropes for wide gorges –

Monkey bridge: Rope monkey bridges are common in the Himalaya and other areas with wide rivers or deep gorges. This type of bridge uses three ropes to span the gap. Some may also make use of additional rope and lacing of the 'V' between walking rope and handrails to make it more stable.

A simple, well-anchored X-frame at least 2m (6½ft) high that is thoroughly shear-lashed (see p49) in the middle is all that is required at each end of the bridge. In order to create this bridge you need a person or team on both sides of the gap.

Lash a crosspiece fairly low down across the legs of each X-frame and dig the legs firmly into the ground if possible to increase stability. Push the X-frame up to about 45 degrees

and anchor the crosspiece of each X-frame to sturdy stakes or trees. Span your thickest rope(s) from a solid anchor a few metres back from the X-frame over the middle of the X's. This serves as the walking rope.

Place some sacking or material under the rope on the X of the frame to prevent it wearing through as it moves under the weight of the group. Then push the X-frames fully upright to tension this rope. Attach your handrail ropes to the upper arms of each X and tension them back to suitable anchors. Adjust the tension of

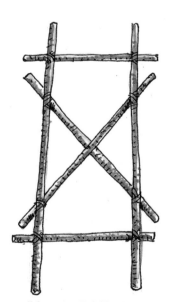

H-frame trestle bridge design

Trestle bridge

much like the monkey bridge. In the latter, safety handrails would then be essential. The side trestles should preferably be dug into the side banks and can be further supported from anchored A-frames higher up on the banks if necessary.

Use long strong poles to make the legs (uprights) of each trestle. Join the base of each trestle with one pole (the ledger) and the top via another pole (the transom). Strengthen the trestle with diagonal braces that run from the outside of one upright to the inside of the other. Join the two trestles together with some load-bearing poles that run from transom to transom. Make sure that the poles overlap the transoms sufficiently to allow for some flex and movement. Finally, place crosspieces over the load-bearing poles to form a smooth walking surface.

If the bridge has a long span it may be necessary to place one or more A-trestles in the middle. Make these by placing two long trestles together so that the tops meet at an angle of 20–30° in the centre of the span, then lash them into place. Strengthen and hold the legs of the A in place by using cross or diagonal poles. Note that it is often necessary to place this supporting trestle in the middle of a river or stream. If possible you should lash all poles firmly in place to avoid any movement.

Flotation and boat safety

A raft is useful as it can be used to ferry small children, aged or injured members as well as supplies across a wide, slow river.

Rafts can be made from logs or from thick bamboo. If timber is wet it may cause your raft to float partially submerged. However, it is still possible to use this raft. In planning the building of a raft, take into account the intended load and make your craft large enough to cope with it.

Raft building

Although there are many ways to build a raft, the most effective method to prevent poles from slipping out of place is to notch them where they cross. Make the lashings as tight as possible and keep the logs from moving around by placing a second pole across the ends and then lashing them into place.

It is always wise to build the raft close to the bank as it will probably be heavier than you anticipate. Launch the raft with the aid of poles as levers. (Remember to always check beforehand that you have tied the raft to a tree or rock – this will prevent it from drifting away after it has been launched.)

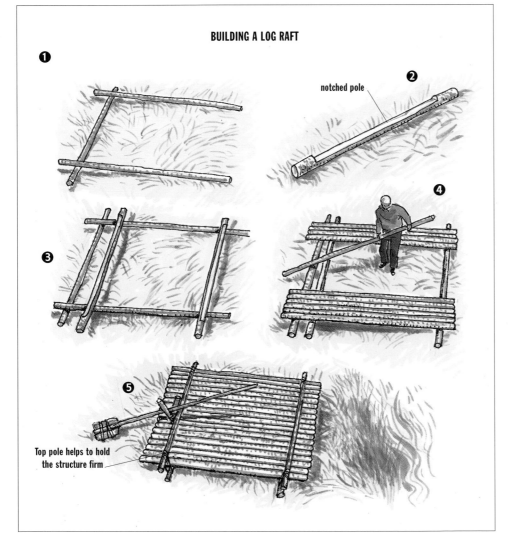

BUILDING A LOG RAFT

❶

❷ notched pole

❸

❹

❺ Top pole helps to hold the structure firm

ABOVE These makeshift oars can be as effective in the water as the commercially produced oar seen here. Make all lashings as tight as possible.

Putting the pieces together

Oars: These take various forms and can double as rudders. If there are no large, flat pieces of wood available, make a broader rudder by lashing numerous small pieces together. (The rudder can be fastened to the rear of the raft by means of a small X-frame lashed to the back spars.)
Sails: If the wind blows in a favourable direction, a sail can save effort and speed up a journey. Once again, you will need to be innovative. Constructing the sail so that you are able to angle it as well as raise and lower it lets you take advantage of differing wind directions. Two small sails (one on each side) add versatility and mean you can use smaller pieces of material. Even big towels can form useful sails. The mast and support beams can be anchored to the base via small logs set in a square.

Dugout canoes: It is very difficult to make a dugout canoe from a tree trunk. However, if you have the tools, sufficient time and large soft logs, then this could be a good option for crossing or travelling on rivers, lakes or even the sea.

Stability in a dugout is achieved by making the base broader and thicker and the sides relatively thin. A tapered, elevated nose ensures that it moves easily through the water.

Sea anchors

Sea anchors, used to keep the nose of a craft into the wind and waves, are very valuable in high seas and heavy winds. In addition, they reduce drift, making it easier for searchers to locate your craft.

In fast-flowing rivers, a sea anchor reduces speed and helps to maintain direction. It can be made from a bucket, an old tube or any piece of tough material sewn into a funnel shape. Even a log can be used if you have nothing else available.

Items such as rolled-up foam mattresses, chunks of wood or empty bottles can be used as flotation aids. If ditched in turbulent water, look around for anything, however small, that will help keep you afloat.

A log tied to the back of a boat makes an effective sea anchor.

Travel in different terrain

Mountain terrain

Many wilderness and outdoor adventure experiences involve travelling into mountainous terrain, while small and large aeroplane crashes in mountain areas are a fairly common occurrence. Mountains pose unique problems and dangers – especially those encased in snow and ice. High winds, cold, avalanches and steep mountain slopes all constitute hazards, particularly if members are stressed and exhausted. Only tackle these conditions if you have no other choice and the only route to safety lies across and down the mountain. It may well be more risky to climb than to wait for rescue. You can only make this judgement if you find yourself in this predicament.

Tackling mountain slopes

What may seem an easy slope to an experienced alpine climber can be a terrifying and dangerous one for a novice. Descent is more difficult than ascent because you cannot pick out good spots for your feet as you instinctively do when climbing up.

If you have to cross steep, snow-covered slopes and do not have a rope or climbing gear, send the strongest member ahead, preferably with a sharpened stick for support. He or she should trample out a ledge for others to follow. Moving across a slope is easier if you have a pole or stick for support on the uphill slope. When walking across a slope, don't lean far into it – you'll be off balance and your feet could easily slip.

Try instead to walk 'on balance' – as straight up as possible. Descending a steep slope is best done in a gradual zigzag pattern by kicking holes or steps and standing in them with your heels. When turning corners, it is very useful to have a sturdy pole or stick for support. If the slope gets very steep, it is easier to descend backwards, facing the slope, kicking your toes in and digging your hands in as you go. If you do not have gloves, use a pair of socks on your hands to prevent frostbite (see p117).

Using ropes and harnesses

A rope is of limited value without proper training and a good set of equipment. Over-confidence or over-reliance on ropes can cause accidents. It is best to practise the elements of rope usage (described below and on p98), which focus on the emergency use of ropes. If possible, attend a registered climbing course offered by a reputable climbing instructor or training school before you embark on a trip to a steep mountain area. Modern alpine climbers seldom make use of only a rope – their climbing equipment also includes harnesses, carabiners, slings and protection gear.

Anchoring the rope and belayer

A rope can only provide security if it is properly anchored and 'belayed'. It can then be used safely to help people up steep sections or to lower them down others. Note that anchor points must be solid and tied off with a figure-of-eight knot (see pp48–49).

The belayer is tied on to the anchor and holds the rope around his waist, controlling any fall by the friction of pulling it tightly around his body. The anchor, the belayer and the rope to the climber should lie in as straight a line as possible.

When climbing, never let go of the belay rope for even a fraction of a second. During a mountain descent, the last person can slide down the

BELOW A mountain guide checks that his client's harness fastening and knots are secure before climbing. **BOTTOM** A figure-of-eight knot tied off with a stopper knot at the anchor point of this climbing harness is the usual choice of climbers.

climbing techniques

TOP A safety rope is always advised for abseiling.
BELOW A friction hitch knot

ABOVE A traditional (classic) abseil needs practice as well as suitable clothing to avoid rope burns to the neck and groin area.

rope if he/she knows how to do so. This climbing technique, known as 'abseiling' (rappelling) allows for the last person to come down a doubled rope. If the rope is placed correctly, you will be able to pull it down for later use.

Abseiling is a dangerous technique, especially when you only use a rope (see diagram below) and you have not had sufficient practice. This technique is suitable for mildly angled descents and should *not* ever be attempted on vertical or overhanging rock. As the lower hand controls the speed by creating friction around the body, do not try to support yourself with your upper hand. Also, remember to pad the neck area to prevent rope burns on your neck.

Improvised harnesses

Climbing with a rope around your waist is not only very uncomfortable, but also means that you are permanently linked to the rope. A climbing harness tied around the waist is a useful alternative, especially for children, elderly or injured climbers. A modified harness can be made from slings, webbing, safety belts or from other pieces of rope. The harness should be strong and be arranged to ensure that the point of attachment is higher than the person's waist.

A 'safety rail' – made simply by tying knots or loops at intervals in a rope – can be very helpful for novice climbers to grab onto. The rope rail can even be used as handy footholds or 'steps' when climbing up or down steeper slopes.

A carabiner with a locking gate (screwgate) is safer than a plain-gate version.

Carabiners

If you have a screwgate carabiner (the metal snaplinks used to connect ropes and other climbing gear), then you can belay safely using a friction hitch knot (see below left). The advantage of this knot is that it allows you to take in slack without your body needing to be part of the belay. When reversed through the carabiner, the same knot can also be used for lowering people or objects that are tied to the rope.

Travelling on glaciers and avalanches

If there is any chance that a glacier has hidden crevasses (deep holes covered by light snow or snow bridges), then a group should be roped together 6–10m (20–30ft) apart with the rope kept fairly taut. The leader goes ahead, testing the snow with ski poles or an ice axe. Should anyone fall into a crevasse, the other members should fall down, dig in their heels, and try to brake his fall. Use whatever techniques you can to haul the person out of the crevasse as soon as possible. Reduce friction on the rope by padding the rope where it cuts into the crevasse.

It is not advisable to travel across steeply sloping ice fields without using crampons (toothed spikes that fasten on a climber's boots) and an ice axe unless you have considerable climbing experience.

AVALANCHE SURVIVAL

- If you get caught in an avalanche, try to move to the surface or the side by making vigorous 'swimming' movements with your hands and feet.
- As you feel the avalanche starting to slow down (indicated when the downward momentum starts to decrease), pummel the snow around you with your hands, legs and arms to create an air space. Lie still – if you can see light, you might be near the surface.
- Listen carefully for sounds of rescue and shout ONLY when rescuers are very close.
- If no rescue arrives within a few minutes, then dig upward.
- Letting saliva dribble out of your mouth will help you find up and down direction.
- Rest frequently and continue listening for voices or sounds of a rescue team.
- If you see someone else caught in an avalanche, try to keep watching them as long as possible.
- When the avalanche stops, move to the point where they were last seen and then search rapidly downhill.
- Shout at intervals and listen in total silence for any faint reply. If you have long thin sticks, use them to prod in the snow for the victim(s).
- This initial fast search is vital. Records show that 50 per cent of avalanche victims who survive free themselves, 40 per cent are found in 'hasty' searches by their group members, while only 10 per cent are found in later organized searches led by rescue parties.

Beware of avalanches

Avalanches occur most often after large fresh snowfalls and on convex slopes of between 30–45°. The potential of an avalanche usually increases when snow that has bonded with underlying layers is loosened by light rain or a rapid rise in temperature. As gullies and mountain valleys can be avalanche runnels (pathways), be especially careful when crossing or using them. Also remember to look for traces of debris below these areas to establish whether they are prone to avalanches or not. If you plan to visit snow-covered areas, it is clearly in your best interests to read up more about avalanche dangers.

Large snowballs running down slopes and cracks or hearing noises when crossing an ice-covered slope are common danger signs of an area that is avalanche-prone. Ensure that you only climb on or below these hazardous slopes in the very early morning or late at night when the snow has frozen. If you have no choice in traversing a slope that looks dangerous, send members across one by one. If you are wearing a back-pack, always loosen the waist belts and straps – in the event of an avalanche, a pack or rucksack can get hooked and trap you under the snow.

Rescue transceivers are compact avalanche beacons worn on your person that transmit continuous radio

ABOVE Avalanches leave little time for preparation; running out of their path is the best initial action.

signals to assist rescuers in searching for and locating lost people or buried avalanche victims. They should always be part of your kit when travelling to an area where you are likely to encounter heavy snow.

Always ensure that your transceiver is switched onto 'transmit' mode when travelling in an avalanche area.

Getting out of an avalanche

Being buried in an avalanche is a truly terrifying experience. If you find yourself in this position, take heart that avalanche victims who have been trapped more than 10m (30ft) under snow have managed to dig themselves out and live to tell the tale.

jungle travel

Travelling in tropical jungles presents an entirely different set of problems and difficulties to those you will encounter in snow or mountains. The dense growth makes it difficult to move consistently in one direction and may necessitate extensive path chopping. Because there are seldom landmarks in the jungle, it is easy to become disorientated. A compass is an invaluable tool – refer to it often. If not available, try to get sightings on the sun or stars to maintain your direction. Alternatively, spread your group members out as far as possible without losing contact and keep your line of travel by moving according to the Triplet method (see p90).

When hacking your way through dense vegetation, cut plants low down on both sides of the path to avoid leaving stems for others to trip on.

Try where possible to sever spikes of vegetation completely – especially bamboo – as this can be dangerous if someone falls onto them.

Chopping vegetation in the high heat and humidity of the jungle can be exhausting, so change the lead person often. Even though humidity and rainfall levels are high in the jungle, you may still become severely dehydrated. Always be careful when traversing mountainous areas that have dense tropical vegetation – you might suddenly find yourself breaking forcibly through a dense stand of plants directly onto a cliff face or steep drop. Loose, damp vegetation underfoot is also hazardous as you can easily slip down a steep slope.

Check constantly for leeches and other parasites. Never pull a leech off as this can leave a nasty scar that

ABOVE To avoid disorientation in dense jungles or bush, make frequent use of a compass. Getting to an elevated area safely (e.g. up a tree or cliff) makes it easier to scout for landmarks or signs of civilization.

festers easily. Rather dab it with a burning cigarette or stick – the leech will fall off with little or no real damage. Turpentine or petrol can also be used to rid your body of leeches.

ABOVE Leeches are at best a nuisance and should not simply be pulled off the skin. Rather burn them off with a cigarette or a lit match.

LEFT A machete or 'panga' is the most effective tool for cutting through dense tropical bush. Take care not to blunt the machete on rocks or to injure other group members while using it.

CLOUD FORMATION IN RELATION TO ATMOSPHERIC HEIGHT

Cirrostratus: thin wisps of cloud or ice crystals often occurring at high edge of a warm front

Cirrocumulus: globular masses of ice crystals at high altitude; indicates changing conditions

Cirrus: wispy cloud; may indicate a warm front approaching

Cumulonimbus: these enormous cumulus clouds are a forewarning of thunder, hailstorms and heavy, unpredictable winds

Altostratus: bluish-grey layers of cloud that blot out the sky and precede drizzle, rain or snow

Altocumulus: large globular cumulus clouds found at high altitude where dark, grey rainfall may occur

Nimbostratus: thick, dark, grey layer across the sky; ice crystals in upper level. Brings continuous rain or snow

Stratocumulus: tight cumulus layers; showers are possible

Cumulus: 'cotton puff' formations that usually occur when weather is fine. Darkened cumulus clouds bring showers

12,000m/39,500ft
11,000m/36,000ft
10,000m/33,000ft
9000m/29,500ft
8000m/26,000ft
7000m/23,000ft
6000m/19,500ft
5000m/16,500ft
4000m/13,000ft
3000m/9900ft
2000m/6500ft
1000m/3300ft
SEA LEVEL

Stratus: low-occurring layered cloud; can indicate a warm front approaching, with light rain. A darker, thicker, wetter version of this is known as Nimbostratus

Watch the weather

Weather can often change rapidly, especially in mountainous areas or at sea. Updraughts – caused by the movement up slopes of heated air on mountains – can cause rain, mist and snow to occur with startling speed out of a once clear sky.

Clouds don't always signal bad weather; many occur daily, particularly in the morning and evening. Large-scale weather changes are often preceded by the appearance of high clouds (e.g. cirrus or altostratus). These high cloud formations predict the passage of a warm front that precedes the main cold front by a few hours. True storm clouds – called cumulonimbus 'thunderheads' – warn that bad weather is close at hand and that you should seek shelter.

There are other features in nature that indicate bad weather. These include dramatic changes in wind speeds and patterns; unusual and frantic animal activity as well as a diminishing ring around the moon (corona). However, the most reliable indicator that bad weather is approaching will be changes in barometric pressure – provided you have a barometer. A drop in air pressure (indicated on an altimeter as a 'rise' in altitude even though you are still remaining in one place) is a sure sign of impending bad weather. Likewise, a rise in pressure (i.e. a 'drop' in altitude) indicates an improvement in weather conditions.

Making sense of mountains

Mountains create 'microclimates'; they modify the weather in their immediate vicinity. As air is forced up over the range, it cools down (known in geographic terms as the 'lapse rate') by about 1°C per 100m (330ft) of altitude (in dry air) and 1°C (1.8°F) per 200m (656ft) in moist air. These figures refer to altitudes close to sea level. However, this lapse rate of the air tails off to 1°C (1.8°F) per 1000m (3300ft) at higher altitudes.

Mountains funnel winds in valleys and between peaks, which results in very high wind speeds. The sinking of denser, colder air at night can lower temperature in hollows and valleys dramatically – remember this when choosing a camp site. If trapped in mountains where there is very heavy rain, look at the other side of the peak you are on. Local wind directions and orographic (land feature) factors often cause rain to fall predominantly on one side of a range. The weather may play a crucial role; by closely watching patterns, you will be better prepared to face bad weather when it arrives.

MEDICAL KNOW-HOW

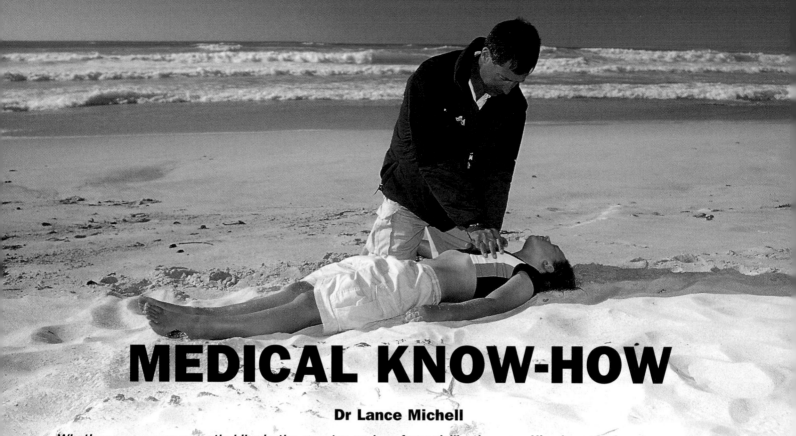

MEDICAL KNOW-HOW

Dr Lance Michell

Whether you are on a gentle hike in the country or days from civilization on a Himalayan trek, once you have lost access to conventional emergency medical services, it's up to you to effectively manage any medical situation that may occur. This could be anything from a minor condition to a full-blown, life-threatening medical emergency. How you respond and what you do can make a major difference to the outcome.

This chapter provides a basic guide in a medical emergency. Those who are not health-care professionals are urged to attend a hands-on first-aid or basic life support course. Choose a reputable training organization that offers at least 16 hours of theoretical and practical training using teaching aids such as videos and CPR mannikins (anatomical model of the body). Ensure that you are recertified in basic life support at least every two years. A better option would be to gain regular practical experience by joining a voluntary ambulance or first aid organization. In addition, serious wilderness enthusiasts should seek

RIGHT A rescuer prepares a young hiker with a fractured ankle for helicopter evacuation.

out a specialist in wilderness medicine to obtain specific training in environmental emergencies that are not covered in conventional courses.

Although one may not like to think about someone in your group being injured or falling ill, it is worth doing some preplanning before setting out on your hike or trip. What are the

likely hazards in this environment? Does any member of the group have a medical condition that could suddenly become a problem? Work out the best way to access the emergency services – is there cellular phone coverage in the area and what are the emergency telephone numbers? Establish which members of the group have medical or first-aid training and consider what medical equipment you need to take along (see first-aid kits pp124–125).

If you are travelling abroad, ensure that all members of the group have adequate medical insurance, including evacuation. Helicopter evacuation can be extremely expensive. Read the fine print as some insurance policies may specifically exclude the activity you are planning to do – e.g. skiing, diving or climbing.

Managing medical emergencies

It always happens when you least expect it. Suddenly someone falls, a vehicle overturns or a lifeless body is pulled out of the water. The situation feels unreal, you have a paralyzing moment of panic, and for a second you pretend nothing has happened.

KEY ISSUE: *How you react and the actions you take can make all the difference in a medical emergency.*

It helps to announce the emergency. Simply stating the obvious, for example 'Peter has fallen' will focus the rest of the group on a plan of action. If you are the group leader your primary responsibility is everyone's safety. A rapid assessment of the situation needs to be made, the accident scene made as safe as possible and urgent medical attention provided. It's a good idea to be polite – barking out orders can be counterproductive. It is better for the leader not to be directly involved with patient care unless he or she is the only medically competent person. This will enable him/her to keep an overall eye on the situation and to delegate tasks to others, such as going for help or looking after other vulnerable group members. Make sure that everyone has been accounted for. The noisiest patient is not necessarily the worst off.

Members of the group who are not leaders should concentrate mainly on working together as a team. If you feel there is something that really should be done, it is better to make a suggestion in the form of a question.

An emergency is not the time to make a take-over bid for leadership. Following a simple protocol helps put order into chaos and gives one time to think and rationalize. A universally accepted approach in an immediate medical emergency is the 'Three H's' (Hazard, Hello, Help) and 'ABC' (Airway, Breathing, Circulation).

KEY ISSUE: *The components of an open airway, effective breathing and circulation are essential for survival.*

If the supply of oxygen-containing blood to the brain is interrupted for more than four minutes – a little longer if the brain is cold – it results in permanent brain damage.

Check that air is moving in and out of the mouth or nose, that the chest and abdomen are moving normally with respiration, that you can feel a pulse and that there is no active bleeding. Action for these conditions is discussed in more detail below.

Spinal immobilization

If the patient has been injured, particularly as a result of a fall or traffic accident, assume that a spinal (neck or back) injury has occurred and take steps to ensure that the neck and spine are stabilized. This means that the patient should lie still and the neck should be kept in a neutral position – not twisted, bent forwards, backwards or sideways. Any movement of the patient should only occur after you have confidently excluded a neck or spinal injury or after you have immobilized the neck with a rigid collar and the spine on a stiff board or stretcher. The only exception is if it is essential to move the patient to avoid immediate, life-threatening external danger. Assume that all unconscious, injured patients have a spinal injury until ruled out by an X-ray. Conscious patients who have no pain in the neck or spine and no numbness or paralysis of the limbs probably do not have a spinal injury.

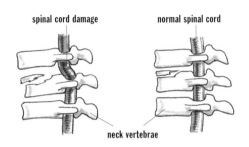

Movement of an unstable neck or back fracture can further damage the spinal cord.

BELOW This injured girl has been placed between some tightly packed items to prevent any movement and to keep her neck and spine immobile until help arrives.

handling emergencies

IMMEDIATE EMERGENCY-CARE PROTOCOL

HAZARD
Protect yourself, others and the patient.

The first priority is to ensure that you, other group members and the patient are safe from further harm. It is so easy to rush to the aid of the patient, oblivious of danger. For example, if on steep ground, first secure the patient and rescuer with a rope if possible and assess the danger of loose falling rocks. Only in an extremely hazardous situation, such as a fire, should the patient be moved without first carrying out a proper medical assessment.

Another hazard faced by rescuers is the risk of infection from contact with blood. If available, don latex gloves before touching body fluids although the major risks – HIV and Hepatitis B virus – cannot penetrate intact skin. Scrupulously safeguard any sharp objects that are contaminated with blood (glass shards, injection needles).

HELLO
Is the patient conscious? Do you have permission to treat?

Talking to the patient serves two purposes. If he/she answers back you know that the brain is functioning and that immediate cardio-pulmonary resuscitation (CPR) is unnecessary. Immediate verbal reassurance is important. If the patient is in full possession of his/her faculties, the person administering first aid must get permission from the patient to treat before proceeding. Just because a patient is injured does not entitle you to start prodding around at their injuries.

HELP
Access emergency services.

Call people around you to come and help if they are not yet aware of the emergency. The question is when one should call for outside help before starting emergency treatment.

In a wilderness setting where help is likely to take hours, a realistic answer to a call for assistance would be 'probably never'. First make a careful assessment of the medical condition and local conditions.

ABC PRINCIPLES
Airway, Breathing, Circulation.

The rescuer should perform a primary survey to check for life-threatening conditions that require immediate attention. Using the ABC approach helps the rescuer focus on the most critical determinants of survival in the first few minutes after an accident.

Airway
Ensure the airway is open.

Breathing
If not breathing, give artificial ventilation.

Circulation
Stop any bleeding. If the heart has stopped, perform heart massage.

VITAL SIGNS

- Pulse rate/min.
- Breath rate/min.
- Blood pressure (if measuring apparatus available – otherwise record pulse strength at the wrist as strong, weak or not felt)
- Temperature if it is relevant (for illness, heat- and cold-associated conditions)

- LEVEL OF CONSCIOUSNESS / AVPU
  - A   Alert
  - V   responds to Verbal stimuli (i.e. talking)
  - P   responds only to Painful stimuli (e.g. pin prick)
  - U   Unresponsive

A casualty with a serious head injury is made comfortable before being assessed according to the AVPU system.

The secondary survey

A careful assessment of the patient's medical condition should then be made. Measure and record the patient's vital signs – the pulse, respiration rate and the level of consciousness. Note if the patient is able to move arms and legs. If conscious, ask if the patient has any pain or other symptoms. Establish particularly if there is any neck or chest pain. Gently examine the patient from head to feet, looking and feeling for injuries. Beware of focusing on the obvious superficial injuries – like scalp lacerations that bleed a lot – while overlooking life-threatening but subtle medical problems such as a partly blocked airway.

ABOVE The group leader stops to check the pulse of a hiker who has fainted. It is also important to measure other vital signs such as consciousness level and respiration rate to assess a patient's medical condition.

Make a plan

Once you have assessed the patient and applied the urgent first-aid measures, the group should consider what to do next. It is generally better if everyone, including the patient, is involved in the discussion. If there is doubt about the severity of the medical condition, rather err on the safe side and try to get expert medical care to the patient as soon as possible. If outside help is sought, it is very important that the exact location of the incident, medical details and all other relevant information is transmitted. Write the whole message down according to this guideline. (see panel right).

Plans of action
Treat

Once you have the situation under control, life-saving measures have been applied and help is on the way, you can continue treating the patient. The main treatment principles are: avoid doing further harm, relieve pain and cover wounds to prevent any infection. Keep talking to the patient while you are busy with treatment.

Medical evacuation

Getting expert medical assistance to the patient fast is a better option than trying to transport an unstable patient in a makeshift fashion. Once a paramedic is on the scene, he/she can stabilize the patient by placing a tube in the windpipe to secure the airway, administering intravenous fluid to counteract shock and giving oxygen as well as powerful painkillers prior to transport.

INFORMATION THAT MAY BE REQUIRED BY RESCUE TEAM

- Nature of incident (e.g. injury, illness)
- Cause of injury (e.g. fall)
- Exact location (use more than one description)
  GPS position
  Map coordinates
  Distance and direction from identifiable feature
  Description of topography
- Number of patients
- Name and age of each patient
- Medical condition of each patient
  Vital signs
  Injuries
  Treatment applied
- Local weather conditions
- Local access difficulties (e.g. patient is on a cliff face)
- Site of helicopter landing zone
- Number of uninjured members of the group
- Group equipment
  Shelter
  Food
  Medical supplies
- Signalling methods
- Medical expertise in group

basic first aid

Until help arrives

Making use of a helicopter to evacuate a patient who is ill or seriously injured is usually preferable if available. While waiting for help, patients must be actively nursed and looked after. They should never be left alone unless this is unavoidable. Make them as comfortable as possible and place suitable padding and insulation between them and the ground. Construct a sun/wind/rain shelter and keep them warm.

Conscious patients can be given fluids, preferably containing a little sugar, in small quantities at a time unless they are expected to be in hospital within four hours. In this case it is better to give them nothing at all in case they require surgery. Help them with going to the toilet. If they are able to pass some urine about every four hours (adults), you can be assured that they are not dehydrated or in circulation failure. Continue to monitor their vital signs in case there is a deterioration. It is most important to continually encourage and reassure the patient. Let them sleep if they want to – there

ABOVE Walking the patient out may be an option if injuries are minor.

is no point in trying to keep a patient awake who appears to be lapsing into a coma.

If a helicopter is not available and you have to evacuate the patient on foot, do not underestimate the formidable task of carrying someone on a stretcher over rough terrain for any appreciable distance. Mountain rescue stretchers are designed so that up to 10 carriers can share the load and even then, carriers have to be rotated approximately every 30 minutes. Makeshift stretchers or improvised sledges are two options for carrying a patient.

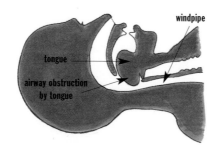

Head and neck airway obstructed.

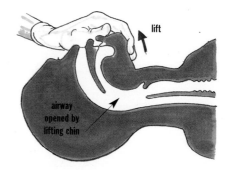

Head and neck airway opened, showing a chin lift. Use this manoeuvre when there is NO neck injury.

However, neither method is suitable if the patient has a spinal injury.

A more viable option is to try to walk the patient out. This is obviously not possible if the patient is severely injured and shocked, has a decreased level of consciousness, has breathing problems or has suspected neck, back or pelvic injuries. However, if you can safely stand the patient up with two supporting persons on each side and a lot of encouragement, it is amazing what progress can be made.

BASIC FIRST AID

Airway

The most valuable first aid a bystander can do for a patient is to ensure that the airway through which he/she breathes stays open. If the airway blocks, we die in minutes. The airway consists of the mouth or nose, back of the throat, voice box and windpipe. While awake or asleep, we are accustomed to being able to do routine actions that keep our airways open – swallowing, coughing and opening the mouth.

It is difficult to conceive that an unconscious person may not be able do this, yet any condition that depresses one's level of consciousness can lower the airway protection reflexes. Without these reflexes, an unconscious person lying on his back will tend to block his airway because the back of the tongue falls against the back of the throat (see diagram p108). There is also a risk of inhaling blood or vomit present in the mouth.

In a conscious patient, airway blockage can result from severe facial injuries, insect bites, swelling from infection, inhalation of hot gases or a solid piece of food that 'goes the wrong way' and then gets stuck in the voice box.

If the airway is completely blocked, the patient will breathe with difficulty for a few minutes and then stop as the brain becomes depressed due to lack of oxygen. When the airway is partly blocked, the patient will struggle to breathe in and snore, gurgle or make a high pitched sound. There may also be recessing (sucking in) of the ribcage and throat.

In an unconscious patient, open the airway by pushing the lower jawbone forward (see chin lift diagram) or use the jaw-thrust manoeuvre (applying pressure behind both angles of the jaw) – see diagram below.

At the same time, the neck should be held in a neutral position in case there is an associated neck fracture. You may have to put your finger in the mouth to remove any obstruction (e.g. lumps of food or false teeth) that is blocking the upper part of the airway.

Unconscious patients should be turned onto their side in the 'recovery position' (see below). Remember to protect the neck and spine while moving an injured patient into this position. Keep the patient in the recovery position even during transport – it ensures that gravity keeps the airway open and vomit can run out of the mouth without entering the windpipe. If necessary, you can make a makeshift suction pump out of a plastic bottle and a plastic tube (see diagram below centre).

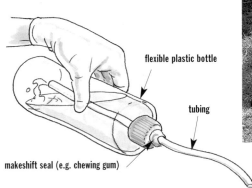

Place fingers behind the angle of the jaw. Lift the jaw forward to keep the airway open. Keep hands on both sides of the head.

Opening the airway with the jaw-thrust manoeuvre (possible neck injury).

flexible plastic bottle

tubing

makeshift seal (e.g. chewing gum)

Improvised suction device.

An unconscious patient should be placed onto his side in the recovery position to prevent inhalation of blood or vomit.

resuscitation

If a patient gets a solid piece of food stuck in the voice box, he/she is unable to talk; however, he/she should signal any distress by making a choking sign at the throat.

In adults, the *Heimlich manoeuvre* (abdominal thrust) can be used to dislodge the obstruction (see diagram).

Stand behind the patient (who should be standing or sitting) and wrap your arms around his/her chest.

Make a fist and cover your fist with your other hand, then press hard and rapidly upwards in the centre of the abdomen, just below the ribcage, while compressing the ribcage with your arms. Repeat this action until the obstruction has been dislodged.

If the victim loses consciousness first check in the mouth for any foreign objectF, which should be removed; then start the CPR sequence.

Small children should first have their mouths checked for removable objects, then held face down and thumped between the shoulder blades to dislodge the obstruction.

Breathing

Having established that the airway is open, the next most important thing is to see if the patient is breathing. Breathing is controlled by the brain – if the heart stops and the brain receives no oxygen, breathing will also stop.

Some of the causes of breathing problems include injuries to the chest, accumulation of fluid in the lungs caused by altitude and after a near-drowning incident, pneumonia or an acute asthma attack.

Heimlich manoeuvre: a rapid upward thrust below the ribs might dislodge a blockage. The patient is signalling with a choking sign that he cannot breathe.

The normal resting breath rate for an adult is 15 to 25 breaths per minute. More than 30 breaths per minute may be an indication of a breathing problem.

Always assume that breathing difficulties are serious and get help promptly. Let the patient sit up if he/she is more comfortable that way. Give oxygen if available.

Stopped heart – cardiopulmonary resuscitation

Cardiopulmonary resuscitation (CPR) is best learnt on a training course and it is beyond the scope of this manual to describe the procedure in detail (see key points in fact panel on p108).

While CPR has saved many lives, one must be realistic about the likely outcome. Even with expert help arriving within minutes and rapid admission to hospital, survival is unlikely. While resuscitation efforts should be performed promptly and proficiently, it should be recognized

Mouth-to-mouth breathing showing the chin lift. Seal the lips around the mouth and nose, then blow gently. Check for a rise in the chest.

that CPR offers a slight chance of survival to a patient with cardiac arrest as opposed to no chance at all.

In cardiac arrests resulting from injury (especially head injuries or bleeding), survival is very unlikely unless the arrest is caused by short-term airway obstruction.

CPR: rhythmic heart compression – thrust down in the centre of the patient's chest, keeping arms straight.

In the wilderness, situations where CPR may save a life are cardiac arrest from hypothermia, near-drowning and lightning strike.

Standard guidelines recommend that unless the pulse returns, CPR must be continued until professional help arrives or until the rescuers are exhausted. If you are out in the wilderness and medical help is hours away, you will have to decide yourself when to stop. Survival after more than 15 minutes of CPR is very unlikely. Except in cases of hypothermia, it would be acceptable to stop after performing 30 minutes of CPR if there has been no response in that time.

Bleeding

After opening the airway and CPR, the next most important priority is stopping bleeding. If you see blood it is important to locate the source of the bleeding. Bleeding must be controlled by applying firm direct pressure on the bleeding site. Preferably use a sterile wound dressing but any reasonably clean piece of cloth, or even your hand (or the patient's hand) will do.

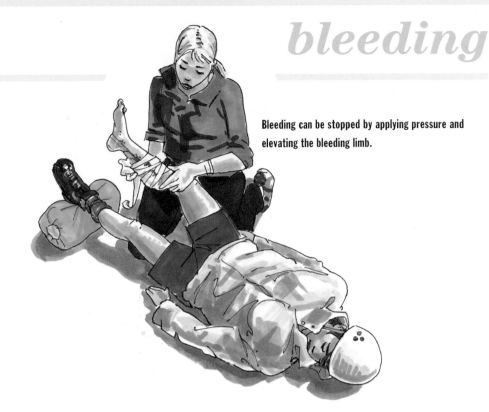

Bleeding can be stopped by applying pressure and elevating the bleeding limb.

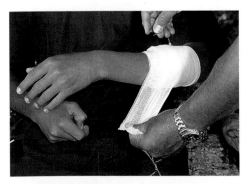

Stop bleeding by applying direct pressure on the wound and using a bandage to maintain the pressure.

You need to press very hard to stop arterial bleeding. Use your hand to apply direct pressure on the dressing for at least three minutes, then maintain the pressure with a bandage. If the dressing and bandage become soaked with blood, apply a second dressing over the first one. Also elevate the bleeding point and check that there are no constrictions around the limb above the bleeding point (e.g. a rolled-up trouser leg), which will encourage venous bleeding. Pressure points are no longer recommended to control bleeding. Only use tourniquets as a last resort to stop bleeding after a traumatic amputation e.g. loss of a limb from a shark attack.

A healthy adult can tolerate 500ml (1pt) blood loss without ill effect, but losing more than 1 litre (.2pt) will start to cause circulatory failure or surgical shock (which is not to be confused with emotional shock).

The body will try to conserve blood flow to vital organs by reducing the circulation to the skin and limbs.

The patient will look pale, anxious and sweaty; breathing and pulse will be fast. Other signs of shock are that the patient's hands and feet will become cold and it will be difficult to feel the pulse at the wrist. In advanced shock, the patient becomes confused and loses consciousness.

Treat shock by stopping further bleeding, and keeping the patient still while lying flat. Elevate the legs – this returns some blood to the central circulation. Rough movement or transportation of a shocked patient can aggravate the bleeding and cause a deterioration in the patient's condition. Unfortunately, it is unlikely that the intravenous fluid solution used to replace the blood lost will be available to you; it also requires skill to administer.

Internal bleeding can occur from penetrating or blunt injuries to the chest and abdomen. There is no way of controlling this type of bleeding except with surgery. Treat for shock as above and hope the bleeding stops.

general injuries

Brain injuries

Injuries to the brain are indicated by some disturbance in consciousness including extreme restlessness. Any period of unconsciousness should be regarded as very serious. One danger is that bleeding inside the skull may compress the brain, causing a deepening level of consciousness. The only treatment for this condition is urgent neurosurgery. Always remember that maintaining an open airway is the most important thing you can do for someone with a brain injury.

Fractures

The symptoms of a fracture – intense pain, inability to move the limb and deformity – are usually obvious and can be seen more readily by comparing it with the normal limb. Broken bones are very painful but seldom life-threatening; however, multiple fractures or those involving the femur (thighbone) can cause enough blood loss to result in shock and death. Open fractures (where a wound overlies the fracture) require urgent surgery to clean out the wound and prevent infection. Fractures with damaged nerves and arteries are also more serious. Check for movement of the toes or fingers and for the presence of a pulse below the fracture site.

Fractures must be splinted to reduce pain and to prevent further tissue injury and blood loss from movement. You can splint a leg to the opposite leg and the arm to the chest. Any suitable straight, rigid object such as an ice axe or branch can be adapted as a splint. A good option for hikers is a soft aluminium (SAM®) splint, which is both compact and lightweight. Make sure the splint is well padded and always check the circulation after applying the splint.

Chest injuries

The most common chest injury is broken ribs. These are very painful and cause breathing difficulties. It is difficult for the patient to cough and clear secretions and this can result in pneumonia. A collection of air or blood between the lung and the chest wall can complicate rib fractures and also cause breathing difficulties. This is treated by a doctor or paramedic inserting a thick tube with a one-way valve between the ribs to drain the blood or air.

Treat rib fractures by giving pain-relieving medication and allowing the patient to sit up.

Wounds

Non-bleeding wounds should be gently cleaned with a sterile dressing. Remove any debris and glass if this can be done without precipitating further bleeding, then cover the wound with a sterile dressing. Leave firmly embedded objects for later removal in hospital. There is little point in trying to stitch wounds; however, clean-cut wound edges can be held together with adhesive strips. Patients with wounds should get a tetanus vaccine booster if they have not had one in the past three years.

BOTTOM LEFT A makeshift leg splint can be made by using a closed-cell foam mattress and climbing slings.

BELOW An arm fracture is immobilized using an aluminium splint and sling.

Burns

Remove the patient from burning material and immediately cool the burned area by immersing it in clean water or pouring water on it. The immersion can be maintained as long as practical, as it helps pain and limits tissue destruction. Cover the burn with a sterile dressing or a clean cloth. Do not try to clean the burn and do not apply ointments. Full thickness burns with skin destruction will need skin grafting later.

Large burns (involving more than 20 per cent of the body surface area) can cause enough plasma loss to result in shock. Urgent hospitalization is required for these and other burns on the face and hands.

Sprains

These are injuries to the soft tissues surrounding joints where the muscles, ligaments and tendons are stretched or torn. Sprains will normally recover given time, providing that they are not further traumatized. The most common sprain is an inward twisting of the ankle, which is less likely to occur if padded boots are worn when walking on rough ground.

The best way to treat a sprain is to adhere to the *RICE* principle – Rest, Ice, Compression and Elevation. Stop walking, rest and apply ice, snow, or cold water – if available.

A sprained ankle can be supported more effectively by strapping it with broad, non-stretchable tape to hold the ankle in the opposite way to the direction of injury. Apply the tape from the top of the foot, around the inside of the foot, under the instep, then up the outer side of the ankle and lower leg. This should be followed by a firm, elastic bandage applied over the tape to further support the sprained limb.

Elevate the limb to help reduce swelling, and administer an anti-inflammatory tablet (e.g. Ibuprofen) to lessen the pain.

If it is essential to continue walking, it may be better *not* to remove the boot after an ankle sprain, as swelling may prevent you getting the boot back on. Once the initial swelling and pain have subsided, the sprained joint should be mildly and progressively exercised, with pain being the guiding factor.

Dislocations

Dislocations are serious joint injuries that cause bone displacement. They are very painful and the affected limb cannot be used. In hip and shoulder dislocations, the long bone literally comes out of the joint socket. The soft tissues are always injured and there may be an associated fracture. The limb's nerve and blood supply may be affected and require urgent medical attention.

Dislocations can often be reduced or corrected by firmly pulling the limb while pushing the bone back into the joint. It is generally easier to reduce a fracture immediately after an injury and this also helps considerably to ease the pain.

It requires skill to correct a dislocation properly to ensure that there is no fracture. If in a survival situation it is probably worth trying to reduce dislocated fingers or correct

ABOVE Steady traction using a weight on the arm (in this survival situation, helpers have weighted a helmet by placing a rock inside it) with the patient lying in this position is the safest way of reducing a dislocated shoulder. As it requires skill to correct or reduce a dislocation, it is best to learn the correct technique by attending a good first-aid course.

a recurring shoulder dislocation. In other cases, splint a dislocated limb as you would for a fracture (see p112).

Common medical conditions

Some conditions need special consideration when visiting more remote areas that lack medical facilities.

Heart disease: Cardiac patients should not over-exert themselves physically and should avoid exposure to excessive cold, heat or altitude. It is important to continue taking medication for a heart condition. A heart attack should be suspected if someone has a sudden onset of chest pain.

Treat by giving the patient one aspirin, keeping him/her still and call for medical evacuation.

Diabetes: Insulin-dependent diabetics need access to medication. Reduce the dose with exercise and if food intake decreases. Diabetics on insulin or tablets are prone to develop sudden coma from low blood sugar. Give sugar if the patient can swallow. High blood sugar causes dehydration and a slow onset of coma. Infections worsen diabetes.

Asthma: Asthmatics who are dependent on inhalers must have a supply of medication. The condition may worsen with exercise or breathing cold air. For an acute attack of asthma, allow the patient to sit quietly and use the inhaler.

Epilepsy: Sufferers should continue with their medication. Take extra safety precautions e.g. belay on a rope in dangerous situations in case of a sudden seizure. During an epileptic seizure all you have to do is stop the patient from hurting himself and allow him to wake up while lying in the recovery position.

Environmental emergencies

Heat-related illness

Exercising in excessive heat is potentially dangerous and causes deaths among athletes and army trainees every year. However, most heat-related conditions are relatively mild and serious consequences can be prevented by taking some precautions. The body loses excessive heat by increasing blood supply to the skin; in turn, the skin loses heat mostly by sweating and evaporation.

Most heat-related conditions occur when exercising in temperatures greater than 30°C (86°F). However, high humidity is a more important contributing factor as it increases dehydration and prevents heat loss when sweat evaporates. The elderly, obese and overdressed are at high risk of being affected by heat-related conditions. Don't exercise in the middle of a hot day and make sure you take in enough fluids. Thirst, low urine output and dark, concentrated urine all indicate the need for more fluid. Sweat contains little salt (skin tastes salty because evaporation concentrates the salt) so you only need to take a little extra salt with food. In hot conditions acclimatization develops over seven to 10 days, after which the individual will be able to tolerate more exercise in heat.

LEFT Desert clothing should be lightweight, but shield as much of the body as possible from the harsh sun. Note the water bottle – drink frequent, small sips unless water is in desperately short supply, when more severe rationing is necessary.

Acclimatization increases sweat production; this means that while you cannot reduce your fluid intake, you will lose less salt when you perspire.

Minor heat-related conditions include heat rash, heat edema (feet swelling), heat cramps and heat syncope. The latter is a faint that occurs after stopping vigorous exercise in a hot environment and is caused by a period of low blood pressure from excessive dilation of the blood vessels. Treat by lying in the shade and rehydrating with increased fluid intake.

Heat exhaustion

This is the most common of the more serious heat-related conditions. Symptoms include exhaustion, dizziness, mild mental changes, nausea and headache. The patient may pant and sweat profusely. Treat by resting in the shade, rehydrating and removing excess clothing. Avoid any anti-inflammatory drugs such as aspirin or Ibuprofen as they could increase the risk of kidney failure.

Heat stroke

This rare but serious condition can be fatal. The body temperature can rise as high as 46°C/115°F (normal 37°C/98.6°F) but the main symptoms of heat stroke are confusion, seizures and coma. Some patients may not sweat despite the heat, although others sweat profusely.

Treat by aggressive cooling, fanning and using all available water. Keep the patient in the recovery position, watch the airway and arrange for urgent evacuation to hospital.

hypothermia

Cold-related conditions

Accidental hypothermia

Exposure to cold conditions without adequate protection (e.g. hiking in wet clothes in the rain and wind or immersion in cold water) can lead to unsustainable heat loss and the development of hypothermia (low body temperature). Hypothermia occurs when the body fails to conserve heat, causing mental confusion. Unless the heat loss is prevented, the patient's condition will deteriorate, resulting in coma, cardiac arrest and death. It is essential to be aware of hypothermia and to recognize the signs at an early stage as the onset is insidious. An entire group may be affected by hypothermia to a greater or lesser degree and, as a result, no action may be taken until it is too late to reverse the process.

The body only functions normally and effectively in a narrow band of internal temperature. The body controls its own temperature but the 'core', consisting of the vital internal organs (heart, lungs, brain), needs to be kept at a constant temperature.

Body temperature drops rapidly in cold water, causing muscle weakness and an inability to help oneself.

Clinical hypothermia occurs when the core temperature falls below 35°C (95°F). Normally, the body generates more heat than it requires by general metabolism and exercise and loses excess heat through sweating, radiation and convection from the skin. When the body needs to conserve heat, it reduces the blood supply to the skin and limbs, resulting in blue fingers and toes. Feeling cold induces various behavioural changes, e.g. moving to a warmer environment, putting on more clothes or increasing muscular activity.

Hypothermia occurs most often with immersion in cold water and hiking in wet, cold and windy conditions. It is aggravated by hunger, fatigue, illness and high altitude. High risk people are young children, adolescents, thin individuals and the elderly. Injured and immobilized patients can develop hypothermia under surprisingly mild conditions.

Hypothermia can usually be prevented by avoiding major risk factors and using correct equipment. Wetsuits and flotation devices should be worn by small-craft sailors and others at risk of prolonged immersion in cold water. Immersion victims lose the ability to swim before they lose consciousness. Hikers should carry synthetic, fibre-pile jackets, trousers and headgear as well as windproof and water-protective outer garments. Carry some emergency shelter – a tent or a large plastic bivvie-bag. Don't pressurize unfit companions to continue with long exhausting hikes in bad weather and ensure that all group members frequently snack on

ABOVE Passive re-warming after being swept into a river is adequate for someone with mild or moderate hypothermia. Use any means to prevent heat loss.

high-energy food such as chocolate.

In each hiking situation where hypothermia may occur, a group is faced with a difficult dilemma – whether to push on to secure shelter, or to stop before someone succumbs to the cold.

Exercise generates heat and is a good defence against cold. However, it can only be sustained while there is a steady supply of food calories and fatigue has not yet set in.

At-risk individuals feel intensely cold and shiver uncontrollably. Once signs of altered mental function occur (stumbling, staggering, confusion, mumbling or uncharacteristic irritability), take action. When hypothermia is identified, immediate treatment is to stop, rest, seek shelter and re-warm the victim(s). Confirm the diagnosis by measuring the patient's rectal temperature (this may not be practical in the outdoors), or take an oral temperature. The latter will be lower than core temperature – provided the patient has not recently consumed hot liquid or food. If not, this is a good way to exclude the diagnosis of hypothermia You need to use a special low-reading clinical thermometer since ordinary clinical thermometers only read down to 35.5°C (95.9°F).

Hypothermia is classified as 'mild' 'moderate' and 'severe' (see table opposite). This is a classification for hospitalized patients. There is nothing mild about 'mild' hypothermia in the field or in the water.

Hikers lose the judgement to take care of themselves and immersion victims lose the ability to swim or cling to flotation devices. Unless the

STAGES OF HYPOTHERMIA

MILD
Core temperature 35°C–32°C
(95°F–92°F)

- Complains of severe cold
- Poor judgement, confusion, irritability
- Slurred speech, stumbling
- Uncontrollable shivering
- Cold, blue hands and feet
- Stiff muscles
- High urine production leading to dehydration

MODERATE
Core temperature 32°C–28.0°C
(90°F–82.4°F)

- Decreased level of consciousness
- Shivering may stop
- Muscles are stiff and rigid
- Irregular heartbeat

SEVERE
Temperature below 28.0°C
(82.2°F) – Core temperature

- Deeply unconscious
- Slow breathing
- Slow, irregular heartbeat
- Heart may stop

ABOVE A polythene exposure bag (left) is more effective than a metallic exposure blanket (right). Get out of the wind and prevent heat loss from the head.

net body heat loss is reversed the patient will die.

Ideally, get the victim into dry clothes, then place in a sleeping bag inside a tent that is insulated from the ground. If dry clothes are not available, use a plastic covering to prevent heat loss by evaporation. Reflective blankets ('space blankets') are not much more effective than any other form of plastic sheeting and they tear easily, but at least they are lightweight and compact. Cover the head as it loses heat more rapidly than other parts of the body.

Adequately insulated mild and moderate hypothermic patients will gradually regain normal temperature on their own. The body heat of companions can warm a patient.

Avoid hot objects applied to the skin as they can easily cause burning because of the reduced blood supply to the skin. Conscious patients should be given plenty of warm liquids to replace urine loss.

If the patient is unconscious place him/her in the recovery position and monitor the airway constantly. Give mouth to mouth respiration if breathing ceases; administer CPR if the heart stops. Severe hypothermia mimics brain death, and when in doubt, continue with CPR until the patient has been warmed up. This is usually only possible in a hospital. Admittance to hospital is advised for moderate or severely hypothermic patients who have been re-warmed, as complications may develop.

Frostbite

This condition occurs when tissue freezes and most commonly affects the fingers, nose, ears and toes. Frostbite may cause permanent tissue damage, leading to gangrene and amputation. General hypothermia and dehydration precipitate the condition by reducing the body's blood supply to peripheral areas. Constrictive clothing, tight boots and smoking can be aggravating factors. Prevent frostbite – stay warm and keep affected parts as warm as possible. Always carry an extra pair of mittens in subzero conditions. Frostbitten areas are painful; they initially look white, later become numb with possible blisters, and then turn black. Re-warm a patient with early frostbite as soon as possible except if the affected limbs have to be used to get to safety.

Re-freezing a limb after thawing is worse than keeping it frozen. It is essential to minimize tissue damage in frostbitten tissue. Do not rub affected parts and try to keep all weight and pressure off the limbs, particularly once they have started

ABOVE Severe frostbite can lead to gangrene and require amputation, so prevention is better than cure.

to thaw. Rapid thawing is far better than slow thawing. Once the patient is at a place where he can be kept warm, immerse the affected part in warm water. Maintain it at a 40°C (104°F) temperature; don't let it exceed 44°C (111°F).

ABOVE This hiker's 'sunglasses', made from dark negative film, act as improvised eye protection to prevent snow blindness.

Snow blindness

UV entering the eye damages the cornea, causing inflammation and pain. Symptoms often do not show up for 10–12 hours after exposure. In snow conditions, wear sunglasses with side shields or wraparound lenses. Emergency glasses can be made by cutting slits in cardboard or by using dark negative film.

Altitude Mountain Sickness (AMS)

Acute AMS usually only occurs above 2000m (6000ft), affecting 50 per cent of people ascending above 3000m (9000ft). Symptoms are headache, loss of appetite, nausea, insomnia, dizziness, decreased urine output

and swollen feet. Symptoms of AMS will usually only appear 12–24 hours after reaching high altitude and are caused by decreased oxygen supply to the brain. Dehydration from hyperventilating dry air also plays a part. Physical fitness levels and age do not determine who gets AMS.

Two serious complications of AMS, namely high altitude pulmonary edema (HAPE) and high altitude cerebral edema (HACE) occur in susceptible people. HAPE is caused by the accumulation of fluid in the lungs. Patients struggle to breathe (even at rest) and the lips appear blue. In advanced cases, the chest sounds as if it is full of bubbles and the patient may cough up foam. HACE causes intense headache and a decreasing level of consciousness.

ABOVE A Sherpa mountain guide uses an adapted rope coil method for carrying an altitude sickness victim to lower elevation. The best treatment for HAPE and HACE is rapid descent.

near-drowning

Prevention

Altitude mountain sickness is prevented by ascending slowly – preferably only 300m (1000ft) per day. A large increase in the altitude at which one sleeps is more likely to cause AMS symptoms than the altitude to which one climbs, hence the advice to 'climb high, sleep low'. Try to arrange a few days to be spent at 2500–3000m (8000–1000ft) before ascending further. See that everyone in the group drinks enough liquid. Taking 125–250mg Acetazolamide (Diamox®) twice a day and starting 48 hours before reaching altitude will help to reduce symptoms. Mild AMS should be treated by delaying further ascent and taking headache tablets e.g. Paracetamol (Acetaminophen). Avoid sleeping tablets and alcohol.

Suspected HAPE or HACE is an emergency and immediate descent by 500–1000m (1500–3000ft) is essential. Administer oxygen if available. A Gamow bag is a portable, inflatable fabric bag in which a patient with AMS can be placed. The altitude is reduced by increasing the pressure in the bag with a foot bellows.

Near-drowning

Drowning is commonly associated with outdoor adventure activities, but is preventable. Insist that boaters wear life jackets, that children near water are always supervised and do not combine alcohol intake with swimming. Only jump into the water to rescue a drowning victim if you are competent in lifesaving skills. Rather throw a rope or floatable object for the victim to cling to.

Submersion victims lose consciousness from lack of oxygen to the brain. Some develop a sudden cardiac arrest immediately after submersion, but most struggle and inhale water. If the patient has stopped breathing, start the ABC steps outlined on p106 immediately. Beware of a possible neck injury if the patient has just dived into the water. If the patient is unconscious but breathing, place him/her in the recovery position – he/she is likely to vomit swallowed water – and keep the airway open. It is worth doing CPR even after a long submersion as cold slightly prolongs the time the brain can function without oxygen. Submersion victims are at risk of developing 'secondary drowning' – breathing problems that develop later after inhaling water. Give oxygen and take to hospital.

ABOVE Turn an unconscious, breathing, near-drowning victim in the recovery position to prevent him sucking fluid into the airway (aspiration).

BELOW Do not attempt to rescue drowning victims if you lack lifesaving skills.

Bites and stings

Wearing suitable footwear, being very cautious where you put your hands and feet and inspecting your boots before putting them on can prevent bites from snakes and insects.

Snakebite

Our primordial fear of snakes makes snakebite one of the most overrated hazards of the outdoor experience. Most snakes have a simple philosophy – if you don't bother them, they won't bite you. The majority of snakebites occur while attempting to capture or play with these creatures. Snakebites are seldom fatal.

Snake toxin is designed to immobilize and help digest the prey. Neurotoxins produced mainly by the *Elapidae* group – Cobras (*Naja genus*) of Africa and Asia, the Mambas of Africa (*Dendroaspis polylepis* and *D. augusticeps*) and Coral snakes of North America (*Micrurus fulvius*) – cause muscle paralysis. Snakes that produce this poison are the most dangerous. Adders such as the Puff Adder found in Africa (*Bitis arietans*) produce digesting toxins that are very painful and cause severe tissue damage around the bite. Less common toxins interfere with blood clotting and cause bleeding.

Rattlesnakes (*Crotalidae*) are the most common cause of venomous bites in North America. Their toxin has mixed effects, causing both paralysis and tissue damage. Bites from this group of snakes only have a one per cent death rate.

The best way of treating snakebite is to calm the patient down and avoid any movement which will spread the toxin. Apply a firm crepe dressing to the affected area and evacuate the patient by helicopter if possible.

Anti-snakebite serum is effective but should only be given if there are signs of envenomation ('dry bites'). In particular, avoid any harmful folk treatment remedies for snakebite. You should not:
- Try to catch the snake – the type of toxin involved will be indicated clearly by the symptoms
- Cut the wound
- Give any alcohol, or
- Administer electric shocks.

Suctioning the wound with a suction pump may be effective. Applying a tourniquet will probably do more harm than good especially with a tissue toxin, although short-term use has saved victims from a neurotoxic bite. Watch for signs of respiratory depression and apply mouth-to-mouth resuscitation if necessary.

Spider bites

Many spiders will inflict nasty bites if cornered or sat upon, but few are more than of nuisance value. The exceptions are the potentially fatal bites by the Black Widow and Brown Widow (*Latrodectus*) of Europe, North America and Africa and the Funnel Web Spider (*Atrax*) of Australia. The Violin Spider of Africa (*Loxosceles reclusa*) can cause severe tissue damage – similar to a Puff Adder – but is seldom (if ever) fatal.

Treatment is much the same as for snakebite. Children with a smaller body mass are more at risk from the poisons produced by spiders.

Scorpions

Very few scorpions can cause death or serious harm to adults but, as with spiders, the sting is more dangerous to small children. A scorpion can sting multiple times and produce a toxin that affects the nervous system, causing writhing and jittery movements. A scorpion sting can be excruciatingly painful, and ice applied to the sting may help. Get medical help if any symptoms other than local pain develop.

ABOVE The small pincers and large sting of this scorpion indicate a powerful sting.

Bee stings

Bees may appear relatively harmless compared to some of the above, but bee stings are in fact responsible for more deaths than snakes, spiders and scorpions combined. This is particularly true of the African Honey Bee (*Apis mellifera*) and its numerous hybrid species found worldwide. A single bee sting is only a problem when a patient is hyper-sensitized to bees, perhaps because of previous stings or a natural allergy. In this case, antihistamine medication (injected or in tablet form) will help. Multiple bee stings can cause shock, respiratory depression and airway obstruction from swelling.

After a severe attack, lie the victim down to prevent any movement, remove the stings as soon as possible and apply CPR if needed. Fast removal is vital – bee stings continue to pump poison into the body for up to 20 minutes after an attack.

Bee stings are best removed by scraping them off with a sharp blade or a needle. Never squeeze or handle the sting – this causes more poison to enter the system.

Wasps and hornets
Wasps and hornets are similar to bees, except that they can deliver multiple stings. Escape or shelter from a swarm by diving into water if possible. Antihistamines and mild painkillers greatly alleviate all stings. Watch for signs of respiratory distress, nausea and vomiting, which may only occur hours later.

Marine creatures
These can be divided into those that sting, such as jellyfish, bluebottles and fire coral, and those that 'stick' such as Stone Fish, Barbel and Scorpion Fish. The pain from 'stingers' can usually be relieved by applying vinegar or alcohol to the sting. Pain from the 'stickers' may be intense and is relieved by submerging the affected part (usually the foot, as people tread on these creatures) in water as hot as you can tolerate.

Travel and tropical infections
Many of mankind's most aggressive parasites and debilitating diseases can be found predominantly in the world's warmer regions. From a medical perspective, travelling in hot areas is thus more hazardous than in colder, more temperate zones. Higher temperatures allow bacteria to breed faster, promoting the growth of flies, ticks and other insects. The best way to avoid many of these diseases is to have the appropriate vaccinations and to be careful what you eat and drink. Always remember to tell your doctor where you have visited if you become ill after returning from a trip abroad.

Contaminated water and food
This is the most common way in which many travellers are infected with different diseases. Most visitors to less-sophisticated countries are likely to experience travel-related diarrhoea (gastrointestinal disease). In towns and villages, travellers are usually infected by consuming prepared food, cold drinks and ice made from contaminated water. In wilderness areas, contaminated water is the main culprit. Ultimately, the source of infection is human faeces that reach the water supply. This is caused by poor sewage, inadequate water-cleansing facilities, handling food with contaminated hands, and flies to a lesser degree.

Firstly prevent travel-related infections by using a water source that is as clean as possible (see p54). Only eat hot, freshly prepared food or fruit that you peel yourself. Wash your hands often – especially before eating. People who have a fever or diarrhoea should not prepare food for others. Beware of ice made from contaminated water. Note that adding alcoholic beverages such as whisky does not make the ice safe.

Traveller's diarrhoea is caused by a variety of bacteria and viruses. It is usually a self-limiting infection that responds to rehydration with copious fluids after preferably adding a rehydration powder to replace electrolyte loss. Alternatively add one teaspoon of salt, with sugar to taste, to 1 litre (2pt) water. Medication that slows down bowel motion (e.g. Loperamide and Codeine) should be used with caution. More persistent diarrhoea with a fever usually responds to antibiotics such as Ciprofloxacin. Prolonged infections can be caused by parasites such as Amoebae and Giardia.

Severe bacterial infections, e.g. typhoid and cholera, are also spread in the same way but rarely affect travellers unless they are in an area where there is an outbreak.

ABOVE Boiling water is the surest way of decontaminating river water to be used for drinking purposes.

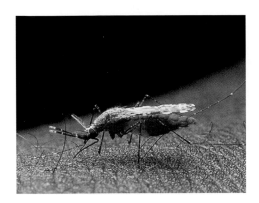

ABOVE Mosquitoes transmit a variety of diseases including malaria and yellow fever. Always take prophylactic medicine if visiting a mosquito-prone area.

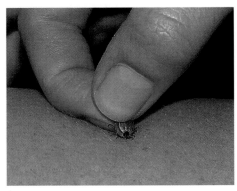

ABOVE Remove ticks with care to prevent mouth parts remaining embedded in the skin.

MOSQUITO-BITE PREVENTION

- Avoid camping near swamps and pools of water
- Always wear long-sleeved shirts and long trousers
- Wear a netting veil over a brimmed hat
- Apply a DEET (>10 per cent concentration) insect repellent to the skin
- Take extra precautions at sunset and at night when mosquitoes are most active
- Burn insect-repellent coils and citronella candles in the evening
- Keep netting doors of tents zipped up
- Sleep under a mosquito net

Disease-carrying insects

Bites from insects can transmit various nasty diseases. The mosquito, which can transmit malaria, dengue (viral infection) and yellow fever, is the most important. Of these, malaria is probably the most widespread health threat to travellers.

Transmitted between humans by the *Anopheles* mosquito, this disease occurs in South and Central America, tropical Africa and South Asia. Travellers are often infected because they are unaware of the risk or do not take precautions. The most serious form of malaria, caused by the chloroquine-resistant *P. Falciparium* species, can cause death if treatment is delayed. Travellers to malaria areas should always take prophylactic medicine. Personal factors and the particular area being visited will determine the most appropriate anti-malaria drug. Get expert advice by consulting a reputable travel medicine advisory clinic. It is wise to start taking preventive medication a few days before reaching a malaria

area so you can switch medication should you develop side effects. In addition to anti-malaria medication, it is very important to make every effort to avoid being bitten by mosquitoes (see panel right).

Ticks are more problematic in temperate climates, where they infect the unwary with lyme disease (an infection that causes chronic tiredness) and tick-bite fever. In tick-infested areas, always use DEET (N, N-diethyl-3-methylbenzamide) insect-repellent lotion and wear long trousers tucked into your socks. At night it is important to search every part of your body thoroughly for ticks.

Blood-borne infections

Hepatitis B and HIV are transmitted by using unsterilized needles and syringes, through blood transfusion and sexual intercourse. An effective hepatitis-B vaccine is available and is recommended. Take a small supply of injection needles, syringes and drip sets along in case you are admitted to a Third World hospital.

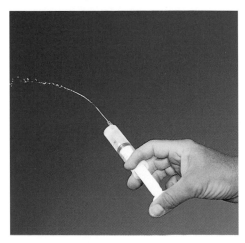

Carry a small supply of syringes, needles and IV equipment when travelling in less developed countries.

common travel diseases

DISEASE & REGION	CAUSE AND TRANSMISSION MODE	PREVENTION	SYMPTOMS & DIAGNOSIS	TREATMENT	COMMENT
WATER & FOOD					
TRAVELLERS' DIARRHOEA Worldwide	Bacteria and viruses Contaminated water and food	Food precautions Water purification	Diarrhoea Mild fever	Rehydration Rest Loperimide Antibiotics	Common
GIARDIASIS Worldwide including North America	*Giardia* parasite Human- and animal-contaminated water	Water purification by filtration or high-dose chlorine/iodine	Chronic diarrhoea, fatigue, weight loss	Tinidazol Metronidazole	Common Cyst can survive three months in water
AMOEBIASIS DYSENTERY Africa, Asia, South America	*Amoeba* parasite Contaminated water and food	Food and water precautions – filter water or use high dose chlorine/iodine	Persistent diarrhoea, blood in the stool, liver abscess	Metronidazole	
CHOLERA Africa, Asia	*Vibrio cholerae* bacteria Contaminated water and food	Water and food precautions. Vaccine is available but not very effective	Profuse watery diarrhoea Dehydration, shock	Antibiotics Intravenous rehydration Hospitalization	Low risk to travellers unless in contact with a local outbreak of the disease
HEPATITIS A Worldwide	Virus Faecal-oral	Food and water precautions Vaccine available	Nausea, fever, jaundice, coma	Supportive Occasionally fatal	New effective vaccine recommended for travellers to 'primitive' countries
TYPHOID Poor African and Asian countries	Bacteria Faecal-oral	Food and water precautions Vaccine available	Fever, headache, constipation or diarrhoea	Antibiotics Hospitalization	Low risk except during local outbreaks
OTHER INFECTION ROUTES					
HOOKWORM (tropics: rivers)	Parasitic worm larva: free swimming	Enters through skin, travels to lungs; adults move to intestine	Pneumonia, then anaemia and extreme lethargy	Mebendazole or Albendazole	
BILHARZIA Tropical Africa and Asia	Parasite: water snails enter skin during swimming in warm, still waters	Avoid swimming in and drinking infected waters	Pain and blood in urinary tract Lethargy Slow onset	Praziquantel one-day course (very effective)	

DISEASE & REGION	CAUSE AND TRANSMISSION MODE	PREVENTION	SYMPTOMS & DIAGNOSIS	TREATMENT	COMMENT
INSECT VECTOR					
MALARIA Tropics, subtropics, Widespread	Parasite transmitted by *Anopheles* mosquito	Prevent mosquito bites Prophylactic medication Get latest info for your region from an expert	High fever or periodic fever, headache, cough, diarrhoea	Pyrimethamine-sulfadoxine (Fansidar®) tablets or Quinine	High prevalence Pregnant women and babies should consider avoiding travel to infected areas
DENGUE Tropical Asia	Virus transmitted by mosquito	Mosquito protection	Fever, headache, muscle and joint pain Tendency to occasionally bleed	No specific treatment Hospitalization is possible	Increasing risk Usually mild 3–8 day-incubation
YELLOW FEVER South America, Africa (tropical)	Virus transmitted by mosquito	Vaccination required more than 10 days before entry to some countries – low risk of infection	Mild fever or severe fever, tendency to bleed, jaundice	No specific treatment Supportive therapy with fluids	Vaccination entry requirement for some countries
TICK FEVER e.g. Rocky Mountain Spotted Fever North & South America, Africa, South Europe, Asia	Rickettsia tick	Insect repellent Tick removal	Fever, rash, nausea, swollen lymph glands	Doxycycline	Seldom severe
LYME DISEASE North America	*Spirochete* (bacterium) transmitted by tick	Insect repellent Inspect body for ticks	Red swollen tick-bite site with clearing central area Symptoms: tiredness	Antibiotics	
OTHER INFECTION ROUTES					
TETANUS Worldwide	Bacterium inoculated into wounds, bites and burns	Wound care Immunization Booster required every 10 years	Muscle spasms Breathing difficulties	Hospitalization Intensive care needed	Immunization essential if possibility of injury while away from medical care
RABIES Worldwide	Dog and other mammal bites	No petting/feeding animals. Immunization after any mammal bite	Slow onset, average 90 days, bizarre behaviour, mania, coma	Hospitalize and sedate. Always fatal if symptoms appear	Pre-exposure immunization for animal handlers only

KIT FOR SMALL GROUP

The following first-aid kit is suitable for a small hiking group going away for about a week to a remote location:

- 2 pairs disposable latex gloves (protection from blood)
- Pocket mask (protection during mouth-to-mouth resuscitation)
- 1 large (300x300mm/12x12in) sterile wound dressing (to cover wounds/stop bleeding)
- 2 small (100x100mm/4x4in) sterile dressing (bleeding & wounds)
- 2 burn dressings e.g. hydrogel (200x200mm/8x8in)
- 1 crepe bandage (+100mm/4in wide) (joint sprains and holding dressings in place)
- 1 small roll adhesive tape
- 1 SAM® splint (fractures)
- Space blanket
- 2 sachets povidine-iodine disinfectant (10ml/1/3oz)
- Low-reading clinical thermometer (diagnosing fever and hypothermia)
- Scissors and tweezers
- Needle (removing splinters)
- Medication (small quantities)
- Paracetamol – codeine tablets (pain), Acetiminophen in the USA
- Anti-inflammatory drugs e.g. Ibuprofen or aspirin (sprains)
- Antihistamine tablets e.g. Promethazine (allergy and nausea)
- Oil of cloves (toothache)
- Loperamide (diarrhoea)
- Antibiotic e.g. Ciprofloxacin (infection)
- Antifungal ointment
- Saline eye wash (.9 per cent) – 10ml sterile sachet

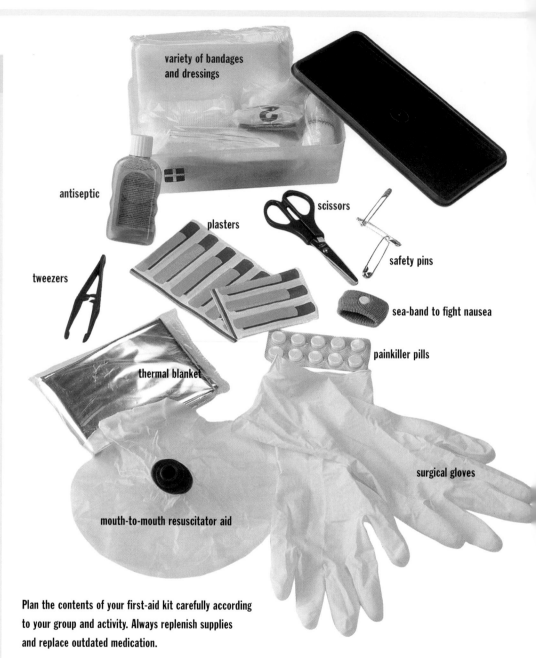

Plan the contents of your first-aid kit carefully according to your group and activity. Always replenish supplies and replace outdated medication.

First-aid kit

The medical supplies you take along on the trip can vary immensely, depending on the circumstances. The most important consideration is the level of first-aid or medical training available. It is no good having equipment and drugs that no one in the group is qualified or experienced to use. Always perform a risk analysis for the proposed trip. Accidents can happen anywhere, but ask whether there are any special risks associated with the proposed trip such as altitude, tropical diseases, etc. Include in this planning any special medical problems that an individual may have. Always consider weight and space

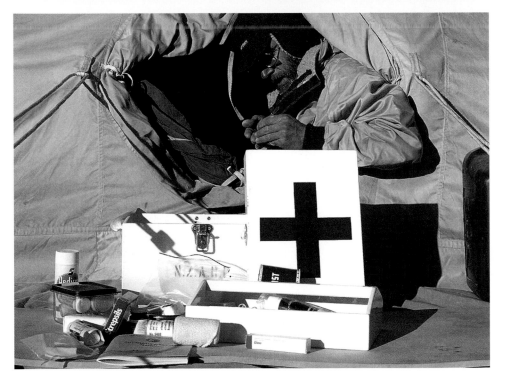

Post traumatic stress disorder (PTSD)

This is a common psychological response to an emotionally traumatic event. Many survival situations may lead to PTSD, such as experiencing the death or serious injury of a member of one's group, being involved in the rescue or emergency medical care of someone who is severely injured or who dies, or experiencing a personal life-threatening assault or rape.

This disorder is characterized by intrusive, recurring thoughts about the experience, 'flashbacks' and nightmares. It can be accompanied by anxiety, avoidance of any reminder of the event, blunted emotions and 'survivor guilt'. Long-term problems include depression and the abuse of drugs and alcohol. Only a minority of people exposed to a traumatic event will develop clinical PTSD, but all will be affected in some way. Failure to process and deal with the intense emotions arising from a traumatic event may cause PTSD. Group members should always be sensitive to the emotional needs of others and should be prepared to listen to others and to share their own feelings. Specialized debriefing sessions held soon after the traumatic event and conducted by a trained counsellor are recommended, although recent studies have not been able to show a long-term benefit. Counselling entails several facilitated discussions between the members of a group who have all undergone the same experience. Long-term problems associated with post traumatic stress disorder may require psychotherapy and the use of antidepressant medication.

TOP This compact first-aid kit includes dressings and treatment for common minor ailments such as sprains, cuts, grazes and blisters.

ABOVE Extensive medical supplies may be necessary if you have to be entirely self-reliant and intend travelling to very remote or desolate regions.

when packing a first-aid kit – you are much more limited if you have to carry everything yourself than if you have porters or a vehicle at your disposal. Choose multifunctional items and keep them all together in an organized waterproof container. Do not include everyday personal medicine in the first-aid kit, which must be kept exclusively for emergencies.

COMMUNICATION
AND
INTERACTION

COMMUNICATION AND INTERACTION

In a survival situation, the most likely scenario is that being seen and rescued will be a top priority.
Once your ETA (estimated time of arrival) has passed, it is likely that in most cases some form of search will be
organized, especially if you have left pertinent details with friends or family members.

How to be seen

A signal is the best way to alert a search party to your whereabouts. Signalling can take many forms, ranging from the oldest and simplest: mirrors, whistles and fires, to the most modern radios, cellphones and transponders. Aim to be imaginative in making visible signs and signals, and make best use of whatever you have at your disposal, be it pieces of vehicle wreckage or materials found in your environment.

Mirrors are very successful signalling devices – over 80 per cent of air search finds have been in response

LEFT Car mirrors are useful for signalling.
RIGHT Ensure that your signals are aimed in the direction of the rescuers.

to mirror signals. If you have one in your survival kit then you already have a useful tool. If not, try to create one by using the base of a cup, pot, or any suitable metal object. Glass bottle bases and car mirrors can also be used as signalling devices.

Having a sighting hole in the middle of a mirror will help you locate and aim it better at a rescue vehicle

(i.e. a ship or aeroplane). If there is no hole you should look alongside the mirror. Place your free hand in front of the mirror so that it partly obscures the aeroplane or ship, shift the mirror until the sun's reflection is on your hand before removing it. Remember to move the mirror in slow arcs to make sure the flash it emits is seen properly.

Signal fires arranged in a triangle at equal distances apart are a universal distress signal. If you are confident that searchers will be out looking for you or suspect you are close to an aeroplane or shipping lane, then pre-arrange the three fires so they can be lit quickly and easily. If there is enough fuel available, keep at least one fire burning permanently. The triangle of fires should be set up to

Signal entails sending six flashes a minute, followed by a minute's wait and then repeated.)

Flares are by far the most effective signalling devices. While any flare will attract attention, red is regarded as the most visible colour. Use flares sparingly and only when you are almost certain they will be noticed. Remember that in any search effort, searchers will probably be looking in a 360° arc. As there is no guarantee that searchers will be looking your way, it might be necessary to fire several flares in quick succession to ensure you are visible. There is a fair variety of commercial flares available. If you select one that fires from a pistol (the Very flare), ensure that you load it correctly – the brass cartridge should be pointing towards the firing pin. Mini flares (including small flare pens) require you to first screw the flare in, then pull a trigger lever back against a spring. On releasing this, the flare fires.

All hand-held flares should be held above the head, well away from your face on the downwind side of your body and craft.

Since all flares can become hot during use, be careful not to drop them, accidentally burn yourself or start a fire. The latter is a risk if you are in a rubber raft or wooden craft.

ensure they will give plenty of light at night or produce plenty of smoke in the daytime as the forward and downward visibility of pilots is limited. Green branches or vehicle tyres give good, dense smoke; by chopping them into small pieces you will quickly be able to produce thick black smoke. Pick your site for maximum visibility. If you are near water, bear in mind that fires made on small rafts and positioned in the middle of streams or ponds in an area with few clearings have been sufficient to alert rescuers.

Material that contrasts with the background is useful to make ground-to-air signalling more visible.

The larger your material, the better. A cross, triangle or an SOS pattern (Save Our Souls . . . – – – . . .) are sure to attract attention. Successful rescue methods survivors have used include controlled burning of bush patches, logs and stones laid in a pattern, and even diverting a small stream to make ponds that resemble an SOS signal.

Lamplight is highly visible at night and is a valuable way of signalling from mountain tops, cliff faces, boats and islands. Three repeated flashes or the SOS signal are universally acknowledged distress signals. (The International Mountain Distress

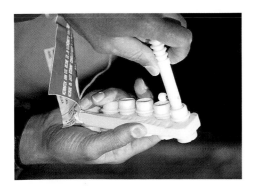

communications

Radio communication

Most small boats and all aeroplanes are fitted with two-way radio systems. Radio is obviously the best way to communicate if you have power and the set is still in working order. If possible send a 'Mayday' (French: *m'aidez* – help me) or an SOS message *before* you crash (if in a vehicle) or are stranded. When the radio set is on and tuned properly, transmission usually takes place

by simply pushing a button on the hand-held microphone. If distortion, a weak signal or low battery power prevent you from transmitting a clear voice message, use the button to send an SOS in Morse code: short-short-short-long-long-long-short-short-short (see also p129).

Many batteries are less effective when they are very cold. If you have small sealed batteries, try heating them against your body. Never warm batteries on a fire.

Modern boats are often fitted with a rescue transponder that sends out signals. Many transponders are linked to SatNav (Satellite Navigation) systems that indicate the precise position. A transponder should always be switched on as soon as you find yourself in serious trouble.

Cellular phone communication

Cellular phones are commonplace and most have an emergency frequency that transmits at a higher intensity than voice messages. If no other contact can be made and you have a cellular signal, try sending a message by dialling the emergency number of your service provider. Another option is to send a short text SMS (short messaging service) distress message via your cellphone.

If neither method is successful, try turning your phone on and off in an SOS pattern. You might be heard by one of the military or civilian 'ears in the sky', which monitor all signals from most parts of the earth. Short Morse code-like signals are the easiest to separate from other background electronic 'noise'. It might

RIGHT Try your cellphone briefly at various times of the day as the range can vary according to atmospheric conditions. Remember to preserve the battery power by turning it off when not in use.

take a day or two before your distress message is analyzed, but it might be your pathway to rescue. If you have the means, try sending an SOS and a 6-figure grid reference (see pp84, 129) via radio, cellphone or transponder.

Preserving battery power

Many sophisticated modern devices such as electronic games, electric razors, pagers and laptop computers have batteries. If you are reliant on a small short-wave transmitter or a cellphone to transmit your distress signal, check the battery's voltage – you may be able to power it by combining batteries from other devices. Most devices need a specific voltage to operate; if you want to increase the voltage, link batteries *in series* to obtain a cumulative voltage, and *in parallel* to increase power.

Small batteries will be drained quickly if used to power a larger transmitter; however, a parallel circuit of several batteries might be sufficient. Small boat radios often work on 12–36 volts (12V–36V), but larger boats and aircraft can use up to 60V (DC) or 110–220V (AC) via a current inverter.

Giving your position to searchers

If you know where you are on a map or you know precisely where you are heading to and want to communicate your exact position to searchers, you need to use a set of coordinates to set out your SOS message. A system of six-figure coordinates is usually used in this type of message.

Example: SOS 157628
(• indicates dot, short = indicates dash and long | indicates pause)

S	O	S	1	5
7	6	2	8	

••• = = = ••• | • = = = | ••••• | = =
••• | = •••• | •• = = | = = = ••

This system is particularly valuable if you are using a lamp to signal an aircraft while moving, or if you are only able to communicate via Morse code due to poor signal conditions.

When in a survival situation, you should aim to preserve all possible battery power for emergencies or for signalling when you see a search vehicle or aeroplane. You might need to disconnect the battery if a radio set is permanently 'live' (some larger craft have this capability). It is very important to keep the batteries warm – place them in a sleeping bag or close to your body (beware of acid from leaking lead-acid batteries).

Limit distress calls by keeping them short – a few minutes – and establish regular call times (i.e. every two hours): even if searchers are only picking up your call signals at the limit of their frequency range, they will know when to anticipate your call in order to trace it more accurately.

Infrared traces
Huddling together in freezing conditions does more than share warmth and reduce individual heat loss; it also creates a large infrared (heat) trace. By using infrared radar devices and goggles, civilian and military sources are able to detect people on the ground. A large heat trace is more visible than smaller individual traces.

TOP A compact radio set is a good investment.
RIGHT Survivors huddle together for warmth and to enhance their chances of infrared detection.

search methods

Organized searches

Getting the authorities to organize and maintain an effective search is often not easy, especially in Third World countries. They do not always have the political will or the necessary resources to do this. More often than not, the persistent presence of friends and family members and strong political or economic pressure are necessary to keep organized search attempts active. If any of your group, family or friends go missing, you may need to become aggressive about initiating and maintaining search attempts with authorities.

Knowledge of search procedures is useful if you are lost as it enables you to anticipate rescuers' methods. For example, shout only during the 'listening' times, i.e. the period just after you hear the search party's calls.

In all searches, the group members should stop and whistle or call every two minutes, then listen for 30 seconds without moving before calling again. This time gap applies to very difficult uneven terrain; however, it may vary up to five minutes on flat, open terrain. If there are several search parties, you should synchronize watches or else all you might 'find' is the other search party.

If it is possible to conduct a hasty search without jeopardizing the safety of the rest of your group or getting yourself into difficulties, then a preliminary search should be attempted before calling for outside help. The sooner you start a preliminary search the better, because the search area often widens rapidly as time passes and the victim wanders further off.

Hasty searches

People often get lost when they move away from the group to relieve themselves or an individual returns to retrieve an item left behind at a previous stop. People also tend to get separated more easily in mist or rain, especially in complex terrain. As soon as you discover someone is missing, you should organize a hasty search. Using whatever knowledge you can glean quickly, you can establish whether to search back along the line of your original route or to one or the other side. Return to the last known position of the missing person. Look for places where the subject could have diverted from the route. Call loudly and regularly but remember to listen between calls. Be careful not to destroy valuable clues that could you lead you to the subject.

SEARCHING IN A NUTSHELL
- *Get all the information*
- *Plan the search*
- *Confine the subject*
- *Search for clues*

Search planning

If your hasty search fails to turn up the missing person, you should act immediately. Even if you think that the missing person is likely to make his/her own way to safety, rather plan for a 'worst case' scenario and treat the incident as an emergency. The missing person may need urgent help because of injuries or being stuck. On the other hand, if he is mobile the potential area to be searched grows bigger by the minute.

If possible, get immediate help from a search and rescue team. An experienced search team will have access to trained and equipped ground searchers, vehicles, radio communications, aircraft and tracker dogs.

Above all, they should have an experienced search management capability. If you are unable to get immediate help, it is up to you and your group to do the searching.

How to start search planning

The last known position of the patient is the starting point for most search planning. Decide, in consultation with others, the most likely scenarios and from this plan which areas should be

LEFT A search team, including a specially trained dog, has been dropped off by a rescue helicopter and prepares to look for survivors. Dogs are extremely effective in locating avalanche victims.

searched. Use a map if you have one. If you have enough members in your group to split into self-sufficient search teams, make sure that each team has a specific task to perform or area to search. This task should be completed within an agreed time period, after which the team must return to your base to report back.

Ground searching is most efficient if you cover natural hazards and the most likely places a person would walk through. Only do intensive patterned searches (see diagram) as a last resort if the subject is likely to be unresponsive and well hidden.

When searching do not merely focus on looking for the person, but also hunt for clues as they narrow down the search area. Anyone moving through the wilderness leaves footprints, damaged vegetation, discarded sweet wrappers or cigarette butts.

Apart from physically searching for the missing person, other techniques can be used to find a mobile person. Place cut-offs or lookouts that will detect the person moving out of the area you are searching. Try to attract the missing person to you, using sound (regular blasts of a car horn), a light in a prominent position that can be safely approached at night, or a line of arrows in the sand directing the person to safety. Leave notes in sheltered places that the subject may visit. Searching can be demoralizing and tiring. Maintain a sense of optimism but do not jeopardize the safety of other group members. Calling off a search is a very hard decision for a search team to make because the person is not found.

An example of a patterned search.

Avoiding being seen

Although being noticed and rescued is a key priority in most survival scenarios, there are occasions when the need for rescue is superseded by the desire to avoid contact with a hostile group or individual. You may unwittingly find yourself in the middle of a guerrilla war, receive unwanted attention from drug or arms smugglers, or as a foreign tourist, have the misfortune of being kidnapped for political ransom by a local group.

If you should encounter a group and you doubt their intentions, observe them for a while if possible. You can learn a great deal by simply watching behaviour patterns.

If you are unsure, rather send only one or two members of your group as messengers and caution the rest to remain hidden. Messengers should preferably be simply dressed, and all watches, cameras and other visible signs of wealth should be left behind. If they are captured or detained, you will hopefully be able to summon help or free them at a later stage.

PLANNING TIPS & CHECKLIST

When planning a search, ensure you have all the necessary information to conduct a successful operation.

- Carefully plan and control your search. Haphazard searching wastes time and resources and destroys the clues.
- Gather all available information on the missing person and the circumstances of the incident.
- Try to put yourself in the position of the missing person – think of various scenarios that could have lead to the situation.
- Establish a missing person's likely behaviour pattern.
- Small children tend not to go far but may become frightened and hide. They could crawl into a concealed place and fall asleep. They may not necessarily respond to their name being called.
- Hikers tend to travel long distances and prefer to stick to paths. If they miss the trail they may blunder on, hoping to make their way back on to familiar territory.
- Emotionally distressed people may seek out a quiet place or avoid searchers.

VITAL INFORMATION NEEDED
- Last known position
- Intentions and direction of travel
- Experience and knowledge of the area
- Full description – physical and clothing
- List of items in person's possession
- Shoe sole pattern
- Cigarette brand, sweet wrappers
- Signalling capability (light source, whistle)
- Medical/mental problems and emotional state
- Interpersonal conflict prior to the incident
- Locations the person could head for

helicopter rescue

How to assist rescuers

If you are part of a group that is lost, it is essential to assist searchers by leaving clues on your whereabouts and movements. This can be done by stopping to build cairns, making ground markers with your initials and an arrow to show direction of movement as well as cutting arrows into trees or bending twigs. If you are sheltering somewhere such as a deep cave, you should leave markers at the entrance. You cannot afford to miss the calls of the searchers when they pass nearby and you are possibly asleep or unconscious.

ABOVE When guiding a landing helicopter, face it with your back to the wind and both arms pointing forward.

Helicopter rescues

Although aircraft are frequently used as spotters, helicopters are usually used for final rescue operations. They do, however, have limitations. They require an obstruction-free entrance and exit path, and cannot touch down if the slope is too steep as their blades will hit the slope (see precautions, p135). Even turbojet helicopters have less control at high altitude levels.

Choosing a landing zone

It is important to choose the landing zone carefully. For safety reasons, pilots prefer not to lower vertically into a clearing, but aim instead for a low-level horizontal approach, usually landing into the wind.

* A landing zone requires a clearing of firm, flat ground with a slope of less than 10° and at least 30m (100ft) in diameter.
* The site should have no high surrounding obstructions such as high trees or large rocks, to allow for approach and take-off at an angle.
* In particular, avoid being anywhere near telephone or power cables as these may be difficult to see from the air and can be fatal to the air crew.
* Clear the landing surface of small, light objects such as twigs, branches and even gravel if possible. If in a snow-covered area, try to compact the snow to make it easier for the pilot to land.
* Give a wind indication – this can be done by using a windsock, a smoke indicator, a large T with the top of the T placed upwind or an appropriate hand signal (i.e. face with your back to the wind, both arms pointing forward – see photo left).
* You can assist the helicopter crew in locating you easily by flashing a mirror or lamp, setting off smoke or other flares or waving brightly coloured clothing (see below). It is helpful to mark the touchdown point with a large H-sign scratched into the soil or made of inlaid rocks packed together (see diagram p135).

PRECAUTIONS AROUND HELICOPTERS

Working around helicopters can be very dangerous because the noise and down-draft caused by the rotors disorient people and make it impossible to shout instructions. The spinning blades of a helicopter's main and tail rotors are invisible and they can easily decapitate the unwary.

- Note that you should always approach the aircraft from the front or side, NEVER from the rear.
- Only approach AFTER you have been clearly signalled to do so by the pilot or engineer.
- Once the pilot decides to shut down the engine, wait until the blades have totally stopped spinning before approaching — many rotor blades 'droop' or drop close to the ground as they slow down.
- If the helicopter has touched down on a slope, never approach or leave a helicopter on the uphill side. This will ensure that you avoid the blades, which can spin very close to the ground on the rising slope.
- As you move towards the helicopter, crouch down and do not have any loose articles on you (i.e. hats, sleeping bags or ropes).
- Beware of holding long items vertically (e.g. folded stretchers).
- If it is impractical or difficult for the helicopter to land, the pilot may hover with one wheel on the ground, or use a cable winch to lower rescue personnel, lift a stretcher carrying a patient or perform a sea rescue.
- The winch sling can carry a massive electrical (static) charge from the air-craft, so always allow the winch to ground or touch water before grabbing it.
- NEVER fasten the winch to a solid object (i.e. a yacht, tree or a stretcher) until requested to because the helicopter may have to break away at any stage.
- If you are wearing a climbing harness, you can simply clip in with a carabiner to the strop (rope or metal band around a block for support) or to both strop shackles.
- If you are using the lifting strop, raise your arms, slip it over them, fasten the grommet (if it has one) and tuck it under your armpits.
- Give a thumbs-up signal before you link your hands. DO NOT raise your arms again after giving this signal.
- On reaching the cabin, allow the winch-man to turn you and pull you in. Follow his instructions carefully.
- If being lifted off a small projection such as a rock platform, wait below the level of the platform or lie flat until the heli-copter skid or wheel touches the ground. Thereafter, approach the helicopter door as instructed by the flight engineer.

ABOVE A smoke flare is being used to guide an RAF (Royal Air Force) helicopter to a landing zone during one of its frequent and indispensable training exercises for rescue personnel.

rescue at sea

Procedures with rescue craft

Sea rescues can take place in open water or from boats with varying levels of seaworthiness. Rescue craft vary from small boats to large vessels and helicopters. In many cases the water is rough with large waves or swells. This could make it difficult for the rescue craft to approach your vessel, particularly if it has loose spars or masts that may damage the rescue craft. You may be signalled to jump into the open sea or body of water. This might seem daunting, but be guided by the expertise of the rescuers and follow their instructions. Ensure that you are wearing a life jacket and that it is fastened before moving into the water. If there are several people being rescued, try to stay linked together if possible.

If being picked up from a boat by another craft, stand at the rail on the lee side (away from the direction from which the wind is blowing) until the other craft draws alongside. Then quickly climb over your rail and try to grasp the rail or ladder of the other craft before releasing your grip.

Jumping the gap should be seen as a last resort. A group should not swamp the rescue boat by frantically jumping or climbing onto it all at once – try to stay calm and approach the boat in an orderly fashion. It is vital that one person takes command to avoid panic and coordinate actions of the people being rescued.

Ladders or nets are often used to rescue someone from rough waters. At the best of times, ladders are very difficult to climb; in turbulent seas they are even more precarious.

ABOVE A hypothermic surfer is pulled onto a hastily organized rescue vessel in choppy waters.
LEFT Emergency flares fired from two distressed boats light up the night sky to show their position.
BELOW Highly manoeuvrable inflatable boats make fast and efficient rescue craft, even in severe conditions.

The best way to climb is to first get a grip through and behind the net or ladder, and then try to get your one leg around to the back of the net. This helps to stabilize you if the boat rolls. Both rope nets and rope ladders are easier to climb at their edge or outer limit with your hands and feet on either side of the net.

Try to 'stretch' the net tighter – push it with your feet, span one hand and then the other against the net and lastly push with your legs. If the boat is rolling severely, avoid climbing up the net if it is hanging loosely over the side of the boat. Try to climb upwards only when the net is lying flat against the boat.

Personal and camp hygiene

Whether you find yourself in a short- or medium-term survival situation, camp and personal hygiene are important yet largely underemphasized aspects of wilderness travelling.

The Wilderness Code's concept of 'low-impact camping' implies that if possible, man should leave no trace of having been in a wilderness area. In a true survival situation this may not be easy to follow, but one should aim towards minimizing one's impact on the environment where possible.

While littering and stripping of the vegetation are some of the more visible aspects of human presence, a more hazardous one involves the biological contamination of soil and water. Without modern sanitation, micro-organisms can multiply rapidly, spreading disease and posing a real danger to your immediate group, to future hikers and to animals.

Wise water usage

Rivers or streams should be carefully zoned into areas for washing and drinking. Ensure that the washing area is always located downstream of drinking water. Any washing soap or household detergents should be fully biodegradable and should be used far from the stream. It is preferable to tip the suds into a pit or scatter them on barren ground. If you obtain water from a lake or dam, do all personal and dishwashing at least 10m (30ft) away from the source. Kitchen waste should be burned or buried in a deep pit. Unless you are in a desperate survival situation, apply the rule of 'what you carry in, you carry out'.

Makeshift latrines

Bodily waste will eventually bio-degrade naturally if given the chance (this is the principle applied to so-called 'Septic Tanks'). If you remain in an area for a few weeks or are part of a large group, mark off and dig a rectangular pit measuring 1m x 50cm (3ft x 20in), which should be at least 1m (3ft) deep. The pit will eventually form a septic system, provided no antiseptics, cigarettes or other foreign substances are placed in it. Do not put any soap or chemicals into this pit while in use and fill it in properly when you depart.

BELOW A carefully planned and well set up campsite is advisable, especially in the event of bad weather. Site tents well above possible flood levels, demarcate toilet areas as well as washing and water-collection zones. Food and kit should also be stored properly to ensure they do not fall foul of the weather or animals.

Two logs set across mouth of hole

rock to raise level of seat

soil

dug-out soil to a depth of 1m(1½ft

Constructing a pit latrine (seen here in cross-section) will make your daily ablutions more comfortable.

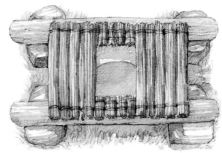

Make a toilet seat by lashing branches together.

EXTREME
SURVIVAL
SITUATIONS

EXTREME SURVIVAL SITUATIONS

You may encounter the unexpected – and unwanted – without warning at any time. A business trip, a holiday, or an outing to visit family can turn into a disaster and then into a survival situation. While prophets of doom tout insurance for every train, bus and air trip, in reality, large-scale disasters and serious accidents are very rare and your chances of being involved in one are roughly the same as being bitten by a poisonous snake. Nonetheless, some pre-knowledge of how to react could prove vital in instilling the confidence you would need to deal with an ensuing survival situation.

In the aftermath of a crash, ship-wreck or natural disaster, people are usually injured, shocked, dazed or disorientated. They often compound the problems by acting irrationally or inappropriately, or by displaying false heroism, aggression and violence. It takes immense self-discipline to be able to regain control of yourself, let alone of those around you. The ability to calmly assess, evaluate, prioritize and plan amid the chaos and confusion remains a vital component in a survival situation. Not all choices are easy or pleasant. Any helper at an accident scene who has had to prioritize the emergency treat-

ment of victims based on saving those most likely to survive (commonly known in medical terms as 'triage'), will understand how distressing it is to make these difficult decisions.

The value of vehicles

Once you have assessed the situation and decided that vehicles do not pose

a threat from fire, fumes or collapse, then you have a valuable resource at your disposal. Most vehicles are generally more visible to rescuers and searchers than human figures in a vast landscape. Possible exceptions are white aircraft or cars located in snow. However, even in this situation you could make the vehicle more visible by scraping off some paint to provide a reflective surface, or cover it with brighter coloured material.

Vehicles offer valuable shelter against the sun and shield against wind, cold and rain. They also contain many materials and tools that can be very useful in helping you survive (see p33). Above all, they provide a sense of security that can be vital to the group in the early stages of a disaster scenario.

RIGHT Despite this plane wreck being barely visible in the Venezuelan jungle, rescuers still found the scene.

140

Unless the vehicle genuinely constitutes a hazard to the group (i.e. it might have dangerously smouldering fires, be in an unstable position, be filled with harmful chemical spills, or sections of it might be in imminent danger of collapse) you should stay with the vehicle as long as possible. Learn to regard every piece of the vehicle as a resource, to be burned, modified or used to your advantage.

In some situations, leaving a vehicle and moving may be the only feasible alternative. If faced with this situation, remember to leave markers that indicate clearly the direction you have taken from the crash site and the route you have followed.

Shipwrecks and sinking

Although small boats often encounter difficulties on large lakes or at sea, larger craft (ferries, passenger liners and big yachts) are not immune to trouble. If you are travelling by ship, take careful note of all exits from below-deck areas as well as the position and type of lifeboats or rafts available. If an emergency arises while you are in your cabin and you are instructed to abandon ship, try to grab and put on as much clothing as possible without wasting unnecessary time. Even towels, tablecloths or curtains are useful as they could provide insulation in colder waters. A life jacket is a priority if you can get hold of one. If not, quickly scan your area for anything that could aid flotation if you should need to spend time later in the water without a lifeboat. Head calmly but rapidly for your assembly point or the nearest exit.

Only abandon ship when clearly given the order to do so by the captain or a ship's officer. If you have some time before the ship sinks, consider collecting as much food, water and other supplies as you can.

DISASTER ACTION CHECKLIST

- **Personal injuries:** Are you injured in any way? If so, are your injuries serious enough to need immediate attention, or can they be addressed later?
- **Immediate dangers:** Take note of any unstable or sliding wreckage, volatile fuel, noxious gases, smoke, large drops or deep chasms. Are any of these obstacles in your way? Do they pose a danger to anyone else in the group? If so, are the people able to look after themselves? Are they aware of the dangers? If not, can and should they be moved immediately? Will moving them put you and others at risk? Can you determine how far away from the wreckage is a 'safe' distance?
- **Treatment priorities:** Must the seriously injured receive immediate medical attention, or should they be left until later for the sake of those who are still fit and have only minor injuries?
- **Special needs:** Are there any children, babies, elderly or disabled individuals who need assistance? Are you able to render this help? Are there others who can assist you?
- **Resources:** Check around for useful items — food, water, clothing, shelter, radios, batteries, lamps, fire extinguishers, rafts, floatable debris. If not taken immediately, will any valuable resource material be lost, damaged or destroyed?
- **Distress signals:** Are there any signals available to let people know you are in trouble; are you able to send a distress signal immediately (i.e. radio, flares, transponders on boats)?
- **Staying together:** Following a disaster, people often tend to wander off mindlessly. Try to assemble any stragglers and ask them to perform simple but manageable tasks — 'Check that everyone's life jacket is fastened' or 'Count the number of children in the group'.
- **Minimize distress:** If a survival situation stretches out into several days and there have been lives lost, you may have the unpleasant task of having to remove bodies from the scene. Apart from possible health hazards, the presence of dead members can have a very disturbing and demoralizing effect on the group, especially the injured.
- **Safeguard resources and supplies:** Make an inventory of all the resources and supplies you have in the group and be prepared to be tough on individuals who might not want to share. This means commandeering all food, drink, matches, lighters, lamps and communication devices on behalf of the entire group.
- **Rationing:** Adopt a 'worst case' scenario attitude and start rationing food and water immediately.

If you can tie the supplies into strong plastic bags that have some air in them, it will help them to float if they need to be thrown into the water.

Water landings

Avoid jumping into the water from any height if possible – rather use a ladder or scramble down. If you have to jump from a height of more than one storey, jump feet first with your life jacket uninflated, holding it firmly across your chest with one hand and your nose with the other. Once you have landed in the water, inflate your jacket as soon as you can, and switch on a signal beacon if it has one. Swim

away from a sinking vessel to avoid being pulled down by the powerful undertow. Look for a raft or any flotation aid (i.e. crates, plastic bottles or furniture).

Life rafts and lifeboats should be launched when it becomes apparent that you are in an emergency situation. Never jump into a life raft from a height as you could destabilize the boat and injure yourself. Rather jump into the water first and then swim towards a lifeboat. As you approach the lifeboat, throw an arm and leg over the side and then roll into the craft. You may need to wait for other fellow survivors to climb aboard while you tread water alongside. Try not to panic – if passengers scramble frantically aboard all at once it may swamp or overturn the lifeboat. As in most survival scenarios, strong,

focused leadership plays an important role in promoting calm and controlling feelings of panic. The leader should allocate positions in the boat, assign people to keep watch for rescuers, ration food and water, decide on the direction if rowing and deal with any sick or injured group members. Firm but tactful discipline might need to be imposed – and you might well be the person who has to assume this role.

If you need to spend some time in a life raft while waiting for help to arrive, a priority is to protect yourself from the elements (sun, wind and spray) and to prevent hypothermia. Put up some form of shelter (however rudimentary), huddle together and bail any water from the craft to keep as dry as possible. If you are in turbulent water you should tie people to the raft to prevent them being

BELOW The end of a long search: a medic helps to transfer an injured shipwreck survivor from a life raft into the rescue craft

thrown overboard or falling into the water if the raft capsizes. If it is likely that a distress signal indicating your location has been transmitted prior to the ship sinking, you should let down a sea anchor. When there is no craft available, then adopt the survival tactics discussed below.

Adrift at sea

Divers, wind-surfers, sea canoeists and even surfers or body-boarders may find themselves carried out to sea in adverse conditions. If this happens to you, it is best as far as possible to stay with your craft, even if it is partially wrecked or over-turned. Any form of flotation helps – spear fishermen should retain the float; divers the BC (buoyancy compensator) and air cylinder; surfers and body-boarders their boards.

If lost and adrift at sea, you need to consider the importance of preserving warmth and energy while still remaining visible.

Taking sensible precautions before you venture into the sea is always the wisest option. The most effective method of preserving body warmth is to wear a good-quality wetsuit if you are going to be out at sea for any length of time, even in relatively warm waters. Many surfers in tropical waters have returned to shore after prolonged sessions suffering from extreme cold because of the dramatic chilling effects of wind on a wet body. Cold and exhaustion, which is often aggravated if your body cools down, can cause painful muscular cramps. These should be avoided if possible as they will reduce your ability to combat powerful rip currents.

While preserving energy is more difficult to achieve if you are lost at sea, it will help if you are warm and have some type of flotation device. Breathing through a snorkel while lying face down and relaxed in the water is a good option for skin divers, whereas scuba divers should float on their back, using their inflated BC for flotation. If on a surfboard or sail-board, try to stay on it even if the water is choppy. Improve your grip by linking your hands underneath the board if necessary and do not detach your safety leash.

Visibility to searchers is very important in turbulent sea conditions. If you hear or see a search vessel, try to raise your hand high above water

and wave a colourful item (i.e. socks, underwear or swimming costume).

Divers often carry small but powerful strobe lights to improve visibility or are equipped with a surface marker buoy – a large floating 'sausage' attached to an air cylinder that sticks out above the water surface when inflated.

Sea canoeists and wind-surfers (boardsailors) who regularly move far from land should always carry a waterproof whistle as well as a flare pen or strobe light.

If you fall off a small craft or find yourself carried out to sea while swimming, you are unlikely to be well equipped to handle the situation. Without wetsuits and flotation devices you will have to rely on your own resources. If shouting produces no response, then save energy and lie in the water. In smooth water, you can float on your back; if the water is turbulent, then turn on your stomach, and try 'drownproofing' – lie on your stomach with arms extended and your face in the water. Raise your head every now and again to breathe; alternate by treading water, then lying relaxed in the water. The advantage of using drownproofing in sea water is that you will not sink; fresh water has less buoyancy and

ABOVE A surface-marker buoy is highly visible even in choppy water and is small enough to fit into the pocket of a diver's buoyancy compensator.

LEFT A Sea Rescue Institute motorboat is a welcome sight to any yachtsman in trouble.

you can still use this method although more swimming is required to stay afloat. If you are in a group, then huddle together to preserve body warmth. Try to stay awake and encourage fellow members not to fall asleep. If you see or hear a craft, splash, shout and wave your hand high above the water.

Makeshift flotation devices

Trousers (or even a skirt, shirt or jacket) can be useful for flotation. Remove the garment and tie the end(s) of legs or sleeves in a knot. Wave the garment over your head to fill it with air, then gather the bottom in and tie it off with a belt, shoelace, or simply hold the end beneath the water to create 'air sacs'. Placing the air-filled garment around your neck provides support, although it might need to be refilled periodically.

Wild rivers and whitewater

The increase in popularity of adventure activities such as whitewater rafting, canoeing, tube riding and canyoning has led to a large upsurge in the number of river incidents. Rivers once considered the domain of elite experts are now being run by large numbers of paddlers.

Don't be fooled by a seemingly placid river – have reasonable expectations about your limits by avoiding rivers that appear to be beyond your capabilities. If your adventurous spirit holds sway and you still decide to challenge a difficult whitewater route, make sure you go with companions who have experience in water skills.

Smart swimming techniques

'Defensive swimming' is the term given to swimming down a fast-flowing river. Float on your back with the current – legs in front – and use your arms to push away obstacles and orientate yourself. If you find yourself in very large waves, try to swim

LEFT Airfilled trousers help to keep this swimmer's head above water, saving precious energy resources.

BOTTOM LEFT Defensive swimming is done by floating feet first on your back down a river.

RIGHT How to avoid being churned in a 'keeper hole' (a dangerous slot formed by a rock or ledge under the water): ❶ use a throwline to drag a swimmer clear; ❷ turbulent foaming water makes surfacing difficult here; ❸ from this point you are likely to be repeatedly washed back to the middle; ❹ by diving deep down, you may get safely past the churning boil line.

away from them to avoid being tumbled in the turbulence. In this instance, it is best to use 'aggressive swimming' – switch onto your belly and swim strongly (still partly feet first) across the flow of the current to move around large drops or head for shallows.

If you are holding onto your boat, get onto the upstream side to avoid being trapped between it and rocks or obstacles. If the craft appears to constitute a hazard, let it go.

River obstacles

A 'strainer' is any dangerous obstacle in the water (i.e. a partially submerged tree or log) that allows water, but not swimmers or larger solid objects to pass freely. If you find yourself heading for a strainer, swop from feet-first to head-first position. This will help you to swim or clamber

ESCAPING A CHURNING 'KEEPER HOLE'

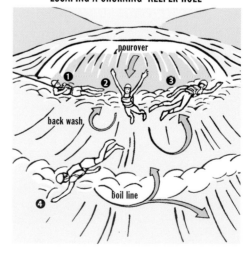

over the obstacle and avoid being trapped by the onrushing water. Do not attempt to go under a strainer as you could get trapped underwater.

If caught in a whirlpool or an 'eddy' (when the current reverses behind an obstacle), take a deep breath, go down a few metres and then swim aggressively outwards and upwards towards the surface.

River rescue

If you are part of an inexperienced group undertaking tricky whitewater you should insist that your group is given some practical instruction in whitewater rescue techniques. Ideally you should also have more than one competent leader or rafter when going on a whitewater trip. Apply the golden rescue rule for a swimmer or paddler in distress – Reach, Throw, Row, Go (Rethrog). First try to rescue the person with a paddle or stick, next try hurling a

BELOW In a raging river, rafters have to act quickly to help a fellow rafter who is tipped overboard.

SAFETY TIPS FOR WHITEWATER TRIPS

It cannot be overemphasized enough – with the confusing choice of commercial adventure trips and operators, don't take chances. If you choose a commercial operator, do your homework thoroughly, get proper referrals from people who have used a particular operator and insist on some or all of the elements below being in place before going on a trip.

- Ensure that all members of your group are knowledgeable and practised in practical river-rescue skills.
- Be heedful of both group and personal limits. Do not be afraid to refuse to run a river section you feel is too dangerous or to insist that a rescuer(s) with a throw-line be placed downstream.
- Also take into account variables such as weather, water levels, potential floods, temperature, poor light and isolation when deciding on whether to run sections of a particular river.
- Check that everyone is well informed on the outline of the proposed trip. Members should also know where they are likely to encounter turbulent water or particularly dangerous sections of the river.

- Check that your craft is properly equipped with appropriate built-in flotation devices and grab loops – they should all be in good working condition.
- If you are travelling in a canoe, the size of the seating area should be big enough for you to exit easily and quickly in an emergency situation.
- Always scout ahead on unknown or tricky sections of the river.
- Establish a clear set of hand signals (see diagrams below) because the noise of the water often precludes shouting.
- Always wear a helmet that covers the top and sides of the head and a snug-fitting life jacket.
- It is vital to have a waterproof whistle attached securely to the life jacket.
- Opt for a good-quality wetsuit to enhance insulation in cold water.
- Ensure that you have appropriate rescue gear for your group (this should comprise at least two sets for a large group).
- If you are going on an extended river trip through a wilderness area, be prepared – take an extra paddle, a first-aid kit and your survival kit.

river rescue

throwline or rope. If still unsuccessful, row towards the swimmer. The last option is to swim to render assistance, but only attempt this if you are a competent swimmer, have rope assistance and conditions are safe for swimming. Do not attempt a river rescue if you are not skilled or confident enough. Rather ask for help from the trip leader or river guide.

Using throwlines
If thrown a line, place it over one shoulder while lying on your back (see diagram above). Grab the line with both hands and bend your head forward slightly to aid breathing. Don't fasten a throwline to a belayer or anyone in the water – the strong current may drag them under.

LEFT Planning and communication are the key to conducting a successful rescue in tricky whitewater.

BELOW Use a throwbag stuffed with rope to learn rope-throwing techniques (left to right): Underhand, Overhand, Torpedo, Side-Winder Coiled-rope methods.

LOST AND FOUND

- As soon as you discover that you are lost and alone, sit down and evaluate your position. Do not attempt to retrace your steps unless you are 100 per cent certain which way you have come.
- If you have become separated from your group and they are likely to be able to search for you, wait on the spot. Whistle or shout at intervals, leaving a few minutes to listen for any response.
- Seek shelter if it is cold or wet or very hot, but try to stay as close to your pathway as possible. If you have a tent, erect it where it is clearly visible.
- Avoid hypothermia by putting on wind- and waterproof clothing before you feel cold or get wet.
- If you move into a cave, overhang or other shelter, leave a clear trail for searchers — you might be asleep or out of earshot when they search for you.
- Indicate your whereabouts by using suitable markers i.e stones (arrows that show your path of movement) or bent sticks (try to orientate them in your direction of movement).
- If it is snowing, build high cairns with rocks or stick tripods to mark your way. Mark them with small pieces of cloth, lipstick, plastic or whatever suitable items you have available.
- Watch where you walk, taking care not to walk over precipices or into crevasses.
- It is especially important to avoid getting onto steep slopes and snowfields, as these can be doubly treacherous if your group is moving under poor conditions.

Lost in the mountains

The onset of a bad storm, blizzard or darkness can often cause disorientation in mountainous areas. Problems usually occur when hiking groups take insufficient precautions or members split from the main group and lose their way.

Key issue: 'When in doubt, sit it out' is the motto you should follow if you get lost in the mountains.

BELOW Using rocks to build a cairn or route marker: cairns need to be fairly large when snow is likely to cover your tracks.

SURVIVAL TIPS FOR A DISORIENTATED GROUP

- Seek shelter as soon as possible, marking your trail as outlined earlier.
- Wait for an improvement in weather conditions (especially those influencing your visibility) before moving.
- When the group decides to move, head for nearby high ground if you have a map, and try to fix your position from natural features (see p80).
- Always remember to clearly mark your pathway for searchers.

- If there is no map available, visibility remains poor, or the nearest high ground is very distant, then move downhill and follow a stream if possible.
- In very hilly country, rather stay on a ridge parallel to the stream because it can pass through many deep and dangerous ravines.
- Be very careful on loose scree slopes as they might suddenly lead to steep drops.
- Keep small children firmly in the vanguard or on a short rope.

Getting lost in the forest

It is very easy to lose your way in a forest as trees often look very similar. Visibility of stars and even the sun can be limited. A forest environment can, however, be used to your advantage if you get lost – shelter from the wind is generally easier to obtain, while fuel and building materials are readily available.

A compass is a very valuable aid when trying to find your way out of a forest. If you do not have a compass, try to create an improvised version (see p83) or obtain location fixings from the stars or the sun. Tree growth can also provide useful clues on the direction of north and south (see also p83).

BELOW Staying overnight rather than pushing on is a wiser choice in a dense forest.
BELOW RIGHT Use a river as a guideline.

Orientation without a compass

If trying to move in a set direction without a compass, you should cut marks into trees as you move and send group members ahead, while reminding them to stay in visual range in the direction of travel. Marking trees will help to keep a line of movement and serve as path indicators for any searchers. In addition, it is useful to mark a few trees with directional arrows.

Set a realistic objective – if you are still lost after a certain number of hours (or days, depending on the circumstances), then consider setting up camp and waiting for rescuers, or taking a break before members become exhausted from travelling. There are few areas where a group with physically fit members would be unable to reach some form of civilization after travelling for a few days.

Consider sending smoke signals by burning green vegetation. Be aware of the dangers of forest fires and remember that the forest canopy may trap smoke. In this case, try to send signals from a clearing where it will be more visible.

Follow rivers downstream – these are generally likely to lead to some type of human settlement.

Lost in a cave

There can be nothing more terrifying than the feeling of being lost and trapped in a dark, confined space. Survivors who have had this experience have confirmed that their largest problem was overcoming panic and trying to stay calm.

Obvious precautions to avoid being trapped in a cave are to take plenty of extra light sources, including spare bulbs and batteries. Be sure to include the caver's standby in your kit, namely, candles and matches or chemical lightsticks. You should also map your pathway or leave clear markers such as arrows or objects for others to see. Let someone know your destination, route and estimated time of emergence from the cave.

As soon as you know that you have lost your way in a cave, you should:

- Preserve any light you have – turn off all lamps, candles and other light sources.
- If possible, sit facing the direction in which you were travelling – this will help to orientate you once you decide on your course of action.
- Evaluate your situation – establish who knows where you are and when they are likely to start searching.

ABOVE If lost in a cave where waiting it out is the best option, keep warm and take care to ration food and light supplies.

- Determine whether the cave is known, mapped, or if new territory is being explored.
- Try to work out how long rescue will take and what resources you have in terms of food, light, clothes and water.

After considering your situation, if it seems more sensible to stay where you are, then rather sit it out and wait for rescuers to arrive. This could well be a better option than getting further and further into an underground maze of cave tunnels. This would only serve to waste precious energy resources and could place your group in more danger from unexpected drops, cave collapses and other underground hazards.

It helps for group members to hold hands, touch one another or sit in contact. This is not only comforting to the group, but also ensures that group members do not split up. An additional advantage is that close physical contact with other members will help to preserve body warmth in the cold confines of a cave.

If there is total light failure, let your eyes adjust fully to the conditions. This should take roughly 30 minutes or more in darkness. Once your eyes are adjusted, use the light of a cellphone or watch to look around you. Be conservative with this light if it is all you have at your disposal. If your supply of matches is limited, try lighting strips of cloth wound around a stick, pen or a defunct lamp to prolong the supply of light (see photograph below). A candle rubbed vigorously onto a cloth coats it, allowing it to burn more readily. (Lipstick, lip salve, butter, cheese and many body lotions or creams are possible alternatives as they have a similar effect). If you have paper, twist it into thin spirals to prolong burning time.

The most agile members of the group should use the light to move first. Stopping and switching electric lamps off before giving instructions to help other members following behind them is a feasible way of progressing in a cave if the ground is not too uneven.

Although crawling in a cave is tough on the hands, it is often the safest option. Use socks or wrap some cloth around the hands and knees to protect them.

As you move along, scratch your initials, time and direction of travel into the ground, or make a marker pile of rocks to assist rescuers or to help you in retracing your steps.

If negotiating very narrow passages, make sure to position the largest person in the middle of the group and never at the back. If they get stuck, other group members will be unable to reverse or assist them.

Moving in total darkness is extremely difficult and dangerous. If you have no other option, everyone should hold hands firmly and progress very slowly. The end (or lead) person should always have one hand in contact with the cave wall to prevent your group from unknowingly doubling back on their tracks.

Forest fires

The first signs of a forest fire might be smoke, smell or the rapid movement or unusual behaviour of animals. If possible, try to put the fire out before it grows too large and gets out of control.

If a fire is already well developed, your most important action is to get out of its direct path. Not only is coming into direct contact with the flames fatal, but more frequently because people are overcome by smoke and gas inhalation.

Fire survival options

In some cases, the only course might be to try to break through the fire. The best way is to cover your mouth and face with a cloth (wet it first, if possible). Choose a spot with a thin stand of vegetation and no holes or rocks to trip you, then run fast and without hesitation through the flames. As you run, be aware of collapsing trees.

If trapped in a vehicle that is surrounded by fire it may be best to remain in it; check that the windows are firmly closed as fire needs oxygen to keep burning. There is a risk that the petrol tank may catch fire and explode but, unlike most action movies, this seldom occurs in reality.

If your clothes or hair catch alight, do not run as this will only fan the flames further. Rather drop onto the ground and roll in sand if possible, or smother the flames with some other material such as a carpet. Use this same method to help others that may have caught alight.

ABOVE Forest fires can move through a large area with fearsome speed. The key is to stay calm, but act fast.

LEFT The primary concern of these rescuers is to prevent survivors from further smoke inhalation, one of the primary causes of death in a fire.

SURVIVING A FOREST FIRE

- Remain calm and do not react wildly; try to predict the spread and scope of the fire before moving.
- Bear in mind when deciding which way to escape, that fires generally move faster uphill than downhill.
- Take note of the prevailing wind and use it to your advantage when moving.
- Head for any natural fire break such as a large clearing, river or rocky outcrop.
- Keep clothing on because it helps to shield you from the flames.
- If there is a body of water nearby, prepare to climb into it as the fire approaches.
- If you cannot avoid the fire and there is no water available, try to climb into a deep gully and cover yourself with earth.
- A last resort is to burn a small area before the main fire reaches you, then move into this newly burned zone which now lacks fuel for the intense main fire.

Hurricanes and tornadoes

A hurricane is a form of tropical cyclone that rapidly covers a wide area and moves along at speeds of 50kph (30mph). Lashing rain and extremely high wind speeds are common features of a hurricane, which has immensely destructive power and can measure up to 500km (300 miles) in diameter. Warning signs of an oncoming hurricane are alarming variations in atmospheric pressure, huge and sudden swells at sea, banks of cirrus clouds, and skies with an unnaturally bright colour at dawn and dusk.

If a hurricane is imminent, move away from the coast since it is often accompanied by huge tidal waves. Find a solid building with a good cellar and close all windows. If you are outdoors, dig into a trench, shelter in a cave or crouch next to an outcrop on the lee side of the approaching storm. Take down any tents if you have time. After a stormy period, the eye of the hurricane will pass by, producing a deceptive calm, followed by a change in the wind direction. You should then move to the other side of your sheltering outcrop.

Tornadoes ('twisters') are small-volume cyclones that develop speeds of over 600kph (400mph). They differ from hurricanes in that the main centre of activity focuses on a funnel tip of only 20–50m (60–160ft) at the ground. Once the funnel fills with air there are significant pressure differences that lift huge objects into the spout and cause buildings to collapse. Tornadoes at sea can cause large waterspouts that may play

ABOVE Wind speeds in cyclones can easily lift you off your feet. Seek cover.

RIGHT A rescue worker aids a distraught woman and her baby during Hurricane George in 1998, Mississippi.

havoc with small craft. If you are near buildings, take shelter in or under the most solid structure available. Close openings on the side of the approaching twister, then open them again on the opposite side. Avoid cars and caravans, which are often drawn up into the maelstrom. If you have no other option, lie down flat in a ditch or next to a tree and hold onto it.

lightning

Dealing with lightning storms

Although lightning appears to strike haphazardly, mountaineers and high-mountain hikers are more likely to encounter this hazard.

The presence of a lightning storm can be detected by fast-moving, dense clouds above; a tingling sensation in the skin; the feeling that your hair is standing on end; and the buzzing of metal equipment.

The best shelter during a lightning storm is to wait it out in a dry, deep cave, away from any walls and not directly under the cave's overhang.

Avoid rock fissures and chimneys, especially when wet, as they provide a pathway for lightning discharges. It is also best to stay away from ridges and summits during a lightning storm. Try to sit in a hunched-up position, with your feet off the

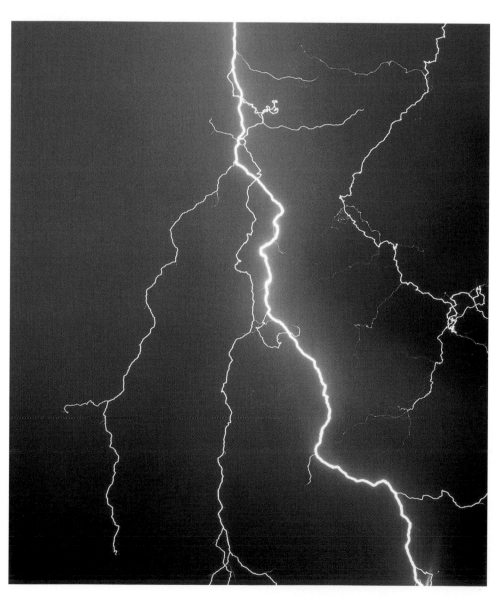

ground, on dry, insulating objects such as backpacks or a coiled rope . If you are caught on open ground during a vicious lightning storm, protect yourself by lying flat on the ground with your arms spread out. This helps prevent you being the point of discharge if the lightning should strike near you.

If someone is struck by lightning, check vital signs and administer CPR immediately. A patient with burn injuries should only be treated later; the priority is to get breathing going and for blood circulation to resume.

ABOVE Avoid chimneys and fissures in lightning storms as they often provide strike pathways, particularly when they are damp.

LEFT Millions of volts crackle in this lightning strike.

Flash floods

Outdoor travellers are at risk from dam bursts and heavy rainfall in water catchment areas that are situated far away. Don't ignore the fact that a flash flood can rapidly turn a peaceful little mountain rivulet into a boulder-rolling mass of churning water.

Nature often provides clues about a threatening flood, such as days of continual rain or poor weather. Be wary of such signs and do not dismiss them.

When camping, never position your tent right next to a stream. Water levels can rise dramatically in a flash flood, sweeping away tents and their inhabitants while carrying large rocks, chunks of ice, sticks and branches along with it.

Always look on the banks of rivers for signs of water-borne debris to gauge previous high-water levels.

ABOVE It is extremely dangerous to attempt to cross submerged roads in floodwater conditions. Avoid them at all costs.

BELOW A hiker caught in a flash flood uses side vegetation to help escape the torrent.

volcanoes

Dangerous volcanoes

There are a large number of active volcanoes worldwide and many adventurous travellers make a point of going specifically to see them. This is not necessarily as dangerous as it sounds, but any active volcano should be treated with respect. In many cases volcano warnings are often given yet unfortunately often ignored both by local inhabitants and visitors. Even without these notifications, most volcanoes provide warning signs. If you are in a volcano region, always be sure to look out for the following signs:

• Heavier than usual escapes of gas and steam
• Odorous releases of sulphur in local rivers and lakes
• Loud noises
• Minor earth tremors
• Sudden acidic rainfall
• Increase in acidity of local water.

Once a volcano 'erupts', several problems manifest, the most danger-ous being ash and gas balls. These dense 'flows' of hot, glowing gas, which are mixed with volcanic ash, are able to travel extremely fast down mountain slopes. If this heads your way, try to get into solid shelter or dive deep under water and stay there as long as possible.

Ash can fall copiously after an eruption, affecting breathing and smothering everything in sight. Volcanic ash can also make roads very slippery and impassable. Showers of ash are usually associated with sulphur dioxide that combines with water to form sulphuric acid. This can irritate or even destroy

membranes of the eyes, mouth, nose and lungs. You can protect your eyes by wearing skiing goggles. Binding cloth around your face will also help to reduce irritation of the mouth, nose and lungs.

Other hazards are volcanic missiles and lava. The former are often fiery eruptions that can sometimes land a great distance away. Volcanic lava flows slowly but inexorably down the

ABOVE Spectators watching a huge ash cloud leaving an active volcano from what is hopefully a safe dis-tance. However, volcanoes are unpredictable, so one should rather be cautious of getting too close.

slope, burying and setting fire to everything in its path. The average able-bodied person can probably out-run most lava flows. As lava tends to flow into gullies, rather head onto a ridge if you cannot outrun the flow.

Surviving earthquakes

Earthquakes give less warning than other natural phenomena and can be devastating. If you do receive warning of an earthquake – either via radio broadcasts or via successive earth tremors in an area that is a recognized risk zone – then take these precautions:

• If in a building, either move to a solid section (e.g. under a door arch) or shelter in a strong cellar with a heavy entrance. Alternatively, move outside, avoiding falling masonry.

• If at the coast, move inland as earthquakes are often accompanied by tidal wave action.

• If in a car, drive away from high buildings to avoid falling debris, then duck down under the dashboard. You are thus protected by the main chassis of the vehicle and not just the window supports.

• If you are in a mountainous area, head for the top or highest ground to avoid rock falls or avalanches.

Coping after an earthquake

• Watch for breaks in gas lines or fuel leaks (do not strike matches in a potential zone). Also avoid live electricity cables, fissures in the ground, unstable pieces of building and loose rocks.

• Do not shelter in a building – there are often strong aftershocks following an earthquake.

• Take extra precautions with hygiene and sanitation as normal services will be disrupted, resulting in possible outbreaks of serious diseases such as cholera.

ABOVE In disaster situations, never give up hope. Here, a young girl is miraculously rescued after an earthquake in Turkey in 1999.

LEFT The devastating power of an earthquake is seen in the aftermath of the one in Alaska in 1964.

glossary

Abseil To descend a steep drop by sliding in a controlled fashion down a rope that is passed around the body or through a mechanical device to increase friction.

AC current Alternating Current – electricity created using a generator (or alternator) or from batteries via a current inverter. Usually in the order of 120– 220 Volts for conventional use (see also DC current).

Airway The passages leading to the lungs, i.e. the nasal passages, mouth, larynx and trachea.

Altimeter Mechanical or electrical device used to measure height above sea level, normally by reference to surrounding air pressure, which falls with increasing altitude (see also GPS for electronic altitude measurement).

Belaying Holding the rope attached to the climber in such a way to stop a fall. Mechanical 'belay devices' or rope friction around the belayer's body or a suitable projection are usual methods.

Biodegradable Materials that can be broken down into simpler substances by the normal action of bacteria, fungi and other micro-organisms.

Cairn A heap of stones or rocks (e.g. a pyramid) used to mark a route.

Canyoning An adventure activity consisting of going down fairly steep rivers, often including jumps into pools, abseils, or tube riding.

Carabiner A metal snap-ring that can open on one side (the gate). Used to attach ropes or slings to pieces of climbing equipment.

Cardiac arrest Cessation of heartbeat.

Celestial navigation Finding one's way across the earth's surface using stars as navigational aids.

Compass A device that indicates magnetic north, usually by means of a swinging magnetized needle. (See GPS for electronic alternatives).

Coordinates (map) System of numbers and letters used to indicate position via reference to those indicated on the sides of a map or pre-determined positioning system.

CPR Cardiopulmonary resuscitation. A combination of mouth-to-mouth (or artificial) respiration with external cardiac massage.

Crampons Metal frames with down- and front-pointing spikes fitted to mountaineering boots to assist one's passage on hard ice or snow.

Crevasse A large and sometimes deep split in the surface of a glacier, often hidden under overlying snow cover.

DC current Direct current – electricity that is usually created via cells (batteries) or via a current inverter or DC generator. Usually low voltage (1.5V – 60V) but of relatively high current strength (amperage). Used to power electronic devices. DC and AC can seldom be used interchangeably.

Distillation The splitting off by evaporation of a liquid at a certain boiling point from a mixture of fluids. Also used to refer to purifying water by evaporating it from a mixture of water and impurities in some form of distillation apparatus.

Filter feeders Small aquatic animals that obtain food by straining large quantities of water through gills or other food-collecting organs.

Frostbite Low-temperature condition in which the water inside body cells freezes, which can rupture the cell walls and internal organelles. The nature of the damage becomes apparent when the body tissue thaws.

Geodesic (tents) Built according to the engineering principles of the Geodesic dome, where a mathematically formulated minimal number of interlaced structural ribs provide strong support to a dome-shaped structure.

Glacier A 'river' of frozen ice lying in a valley that is usually steep. Glaciers tend to 'creep' downhill under the effect of gravity and the increased weight of fresh snowfall found on the upper reaches.

GPS Global Positioning System – a sophisticated electronic device used for navigation that exchanges signals with a series of fixed-position satellites in order to triangulate its 3-dimensional position on the earth. GPS devices are able to provide coordinates, altitude readings, compass bearings and track travel.

Grid North The direction of north given on a map with reference to an accepted convention of N–S and E–W lines for that specific area.

Harness A specialized safety belt that fastens around the legs and body; used in rock climbing and related activities.

Hasty search A rapidly organized search of the most likely zones in which a missing group is likely to be found. Well-run hasty searches have proven to be highly effective.

Heliograph A mirror or polished metal plate used to reflect the rays of the sun as a means of signalling.

HIV Human Immuno-deficiency Virus. Associated with and thought to be responsible for AIDS (Acquired Immune Deficiency Syndrome).

Hypothermia A serious and insidious condition associated with exposure to low temperatures and wind chill. The body systematically shuts down certain functions as a protective mechanism to preserve its core temperature as long as possible.

Infrared (radiation) Electromagnetic radiation below the visible red spectrum. This is conventionally registered and referred to as 'heat'.

Karrimat A generic term for a closed-cell (dense) foam mattress.

Kernmantel rope Rope that has an inner core (kern) and a hardier thin sheath (mantel). Proper climbing rope is of kernmantel construction.

Lashing (ropes) The process whereby rope or cord is used to join two or more spars together.

Layering (clothing) A principle whereby several thinner layers of clothing are used for effective insulation instead of one thick garment.

Lee side The side of a craft away from the force of the wind (downwind).

Lightsticks Transparent tubes – usually made of plastic – that are filled with a photoluminescent set of chemicals and specially designed to generate a moderate amount of light for a number of hours.

LZ Landing Zone – a specific area designated for helicopter landing and take off.

Machete A long, sharp-edged heavy metal cutting blade (about 50cm or 2ft) usually used as a form of axe in clearing tropical vegetation.

Magnetic declination The amount by which the direction of true north differs from that of magnetic north on a particular section of the earth's surface.

Magnetic North The point on the Northern Hemisphere of the earth's surface that corresponds to the convergence of the electro-magnetic lines of force surrounding the earth. Located by means of a compass. This point is NOT at the geographical (rotational) North pole.

Magnetic variation See Magnetic Declination.

Multi-purpose tool A pocket-sized, compact tool that has several blades or attachments. These usually include a knife, saw, screwdrivers, pliers and similar.

Near-drowning Cessation of breathing and possibly cardiac function as a result of immersion in water. Often incorrectly referred to as 'drowning'. The latter term is used medically only to refer to someone who has died as a result of immersion in water.

Off-piste skiing Skiing on snow that is not designated as normal slopes for commercial skiing, which are known as 'piste'.

Quinze A type of igloo created from a dome of hard-packed snow.

Rip currents Powerful, localized ocean currents resulting from landform, winds and tides. Rip currents usually carry objects away from the shore.

SatNav Satellite Navigation (see GPS).

Scree slope A slope covered with many small, loose rocks or boulders, making for unstable footing.

Scuba Self-Contained Underwater Breathing Apparatus. This equipment is often referred to as Aqualungs. Used to dive for prolonged periods of time.

Snare An animal trap made from a wire or cord noose.

Strop (winch) The broad loop found attached to the end of a rescue rope or cable, into which the victim places his or her upper body in order to be lifted.

Throw line A light, polypropylene line that is thrown towards the victim in order to effect a rescue in water.

Topography The landform of an area.

Transponder A device that sends a signal which can be picked up by a suitable (often satellite-based) receiver to assist in locating a group in difficulties, such as an avalanche transponder or a yacht transponder.

Triage The process of determining the priority in which victims should receive medical treatment or be evacuated according to their long-term survival chances. Although there are internationally recognized formats for triage, common sense may have to dictate in some emergency situations.

True North The geographical North Pole (established as the point of rotation of the earth around its axis).

UV radiation Electromagnetic radiation that occurs beyond the upper (blue) visible spectrum. UV radiation is harmful to living tissue, particularly in high doses or for prolonged periods of time. 'Sunburn' is caused by UV rays.

VHF (radio) Very High Frequency radio, also called 'short wave'. It has a much longer range than conventional radio as it 'bounces' signals around the earth by reflecting them from a layer of the earth's atmosphere.

Wetsuit A body covering made of closed-cell neoprene. This material traps water in the tiny 'cells'. Once this water heats up from your body, a warm, insulated layer is formed next to the body.

Whipping (rope) Using thinner rope or cord to bind the end of a thicker rope to prevent the end from fraying.

Wind-chill factor Effect of wind in dissipating heat from a body; this has the effect of lowering the effective temperature below the actual still air temperature. In wet conditions, water evaporation causes the body temperature to decrease.

index

index and bibliography

BIBLIOGRAPHY

BOY SCOUTS OF AMERICA. (1983). *Fieldbook*, BSA. Texas: Irving.

CLARKE, JAMES. (1987). *Earthlink Survival Guide to the Outdoors.* Johannesburg: HCI Press.

CORNELL, JAMES. (1982). *The Great International Disaster Book.* New York: Charles Scribner's Sons.

FYFFE, ALLEN; PETER, IAIN. (1990). *The Handbook of Climbing.* London: Pelham Books.

HASTINGS, MCDONALD. (1975). *After You, Robinson Crusoe.* London: Pelham Books.

LANGMUIR, ERIC. (1990). *Mountaincraft and Leadership.* Glascow: Brown, Son and Ferguson.

MC MANNERS, HUGH. (1995). *The Backpacker's Handbook.* London: Dorling Kindersley.

MC MANNERS, HUGH. (1994). *The Complete Survival Manual.* London: Dorling Kindersley.

NALIPKA, JAMES; CALLAHAN, STEPHEN. (1993). *Capsized.* London: Harper Collins.

READ, PIERS PAUL. (1974). *Alive – The Story of the Andean Survivors.* London: Allison Press.

ROBERTSON, JOANNE; SCOTT, JAMES. (1993). *Lost in the Himalaya.* London: Mainstream.

STEELE, PETER. (1976). *Medical Care for Mountain Climbers.* London: William Heinemann Medical Books.

WISEMAN, JOHN. (1986). *The SAS Survival Handbook.* Collins Harvill.

Medical references

AMERICAN COLLEGE OF SURGEONS COMMITTEE ON TRAUMA. (1997). *Advanced Trauma Life Support for Doctors – Instructor Course Manual.* Chicago: American College of Surgeons.

AMERICAN HEART ASSOCIATION, International Liaison Committee on Resuscitation. (2000). *Guidelines 2000 for Cardiopulmonary Resuscitation and Emergency Cardiovascular Care.* Circulation. Vol. 2 No 8 (Supl).

GUNTUPALLI, KK, HANANIA, NA. (Ed.) (1999). *Environmental Emergencies, Critical Care Clinics.* Vol. 15 No 2 April . Philadelphia: WB Saunders Co.

JONG EC. (Ed). (1999). Travel Medicine. *Medical Clinics North America.* July Vol. 83 No 4. Philadelphia: WB Saunders.

LA VALLA P, STOFFEL R, JONES ASG. (1995). *Search is an Emergency. A text for managing search operations.* (4th edition). Olympia: The Emergency Response Institute.

RYAN ET, KAIN KC. (2000). *Health advice and immunizations for travelers.* New England Journal of Medicine. Vol. 342 No 23. P1716–1725.

STEWART, CE. *Environmental Emergencies*, 1990. Baltimore: Williams & Wilkins.

WILKERSON, JA. (Ed.) (1992). *Medicine for Mountaineering and other Wilderness Activities.* (4th Ed). Seattle: The Mountaineers.

GA – Graeme Addison. HA – Heather Angel (Natural Visions). AB – Andy Belcher (Legend Photography). BDE – Black Diamond Equipment. ABI – Anders Blomqvist (The Seeing Eye). LB – Leo Braack. SC – SKA Celliers. CC – Christel Clear. SCPL – Sylvia Cordaiy Photo Library Ltd (LG – Les Gibbon). DD – Dave Davies. GE – Greg Epperson. MF – Martyn Farr. FF – Ffotograff (PA – Patricia Aithie; MH – Mark Hannaford). FLPA – Frank Lane Picture Agency – Images of Nature (ZE – Zingel Eichhorn; SMc – Steve McCutcheon; MN – M Nimmo; TW – Terry Whittaker). JF – J Fox/Getaway. GI/TS – Gallo Images/Tony Stone (JB – James Balog; AB – Anthony Bannister; JBe – John Beatty; ABo – Andrea Booher; DB – Dugald Bremner; GB – Gary Brettnacher; PC – Paul Chesley; JCo – Joe Cornish; MF – Michael Frye; J&EF – John & Eliza Forder; PH – Paul Harris; KH – Kennan Harvey; DH – David Hiser; JJa – Jacques Jangoux; BJ – Beverly Joubert; RK – Russel Kaye; JK – Jerry Kobalenko; MM – Mike Magnuson; RM – Roine Magnusson; P&KS – Philip & Karen Smith; JS – Jess Stock; TSt –

Tom Stock; MT – Mike Timo; AW – Art Wolfe). BHP – Bill Hatcher Photography. GH – Garth Hattingh. HH – Hedgehog House NZ (LB – Lydia Bradey; BB – Barbara Brown; RB – Rob Brown; PC – Peter Cleary; WF – Walter Fowlie; NG – Nick Groves; CM – Colin Monteath; CR – Chris Rudge; GS – Geoff Spearpoint; GW – Geoff Wayatt). I – Inpra [Sygma] (RF – Rex Features Ltd; TI – Tim Izbell; PIS – Pascal le Segretain; W– Weiss). INC – Independent Newspapers Cape. JJ – Jack Jackson. HL – Holger Leue Photography. LT – Lochman Transparencies (JL – Jiri Lochman; ML – Marie Lochman; DS – Dennis Sarson). JM – Jacques Marais. PM – Peter Mertz. DrLM – Dr Lance Michell. MC – Mountain Camera (JC – John Cleare; CMc – Cameron McNeish; PM – Pat Morrow). NHIL – New Holland Image Library (AJ – Anthony Johnson). NSRI – National Sea Rescue Institute of South Africa. CODC – Cathy O'Dowd Collection. PA – Photo Access Photographic Library (DA – D Allen; P&LA – Paul & Lindamarie Ambrose; GdP – GPL du Plessis; SR – Steven Razzetti; DR – D Rogers; PS – Peter Steyn; PV – Paul Viant/ VCL); [PE – Planet Earth Pictures : TC – Terry Carew; E&N – Eastcott & Momatiuk; DP – David Ponton). PB – Picture Box (RC – Ron Chapple; HQ – Hoa Qui/Manaud). CP – Carol Polich. ER – E Roberts. SS – Stock-Shot (JS – Jess Stock; DWi – D Willis). SIL – Struik Image Library (MC – Mike Carelse). IT – Ian Trafford. TI – Travel Ink (DT – David Toase). DW – David Wall.

ROUTE CARD

AREA _____ DATES _____

PARTY LEADER(S) 1. _____ AGE _____ 2. _____ AGE _____

MEMBERS 1. _____ AGE _____ 2. _____ AGE _____

3. _____ AGE _____ 4. _____ AGE _____

5. _____ AGE _____ 6. _____ AGE _____

7. _____ AGE _____ 8. _____ AGE _____

INTENDED ROUTE _____

_____

_____

ESCAPE ROUTE _____

_____

SPECIAL KIT _____

SPECIAL NEEDS _____

CONTACT NUMBERS _____

DEPARTURE POINT _____ VEHICLE _____

ARRIVAL POINT _____ REG. NO. _____

ESTIMATED TIME OF DEPARTURE _____ ACTUAL _____

ESTIMATED TIME OF ARRIVAL _____ ACTUAL _____

ABOVE As a precaution, fill out a route card such as this one and leave it with a suitable contact person before embarking on any wilderness trip (see p20).

Cover (front)	main	I/W
	top	GI/TS/JK
	front flap	GI/TS/DB
	spine	GI/TS/MF
(back)	centre	MC/JC
	inset	GI/TS/KH
1		GI/TS/KH
2–3		HL
4–5		DW
6		GI/TS/PC
7	cr	I/W
	br	DW
8–9	t	GI/TS/JK
10–11		PA/SR
12	t	GI/TS/P&KS
	b	PB/RC
13	l	HH/LB
	r	MF
14	tr	GI/TS/JBe
	c	DW
	b	SC
15	b	GH
16	tr	I
	bl	GI/TS/GB
17	r	HH/CM
18	t	PA/PV
18–19		MC/JC
19	br	AB
20		JJ
21		CP
22–23		GI/TS/DH
24	t	GI/TS/PH
26	tr	GI/TS/JCo
	cr/b	MC/JC
28	tr	CODC
	br	GI/TS/AW
	tl/bl	BDE
29	t	GI/TS/J&EF
30	tr	JM
	bl	DW

31	bl	AB
32	tr	NHIL/AJ
34	t	TI/DT
	br	FLPA/MN
36–37		GI/TS/RK
38	b	GH
39	bl–br	MC/JC
40	t	MC/CMc
41	t	I/W
	c	SCPL/LG
	b	ABI
42	tr	GI/TS/JB
	cr	HH/GS
	c	HH/CM
	b	JJ
44	bl	MC/JC
	br	GI/TS/ABo
46	b	PB/HQ
50		GI/TS/JS
52	tl	PA/PE/DP
	tr	PA/PE/E&M
	cl	PM
	cr	LT/JL
	bl	GH
	br	LT/DS
56	tr	GH
	bc/br	HA
58	tr	JF
	bl	FF/MH
	br	FF/PA
59	tl	GI/TS/BJ
	tr	FLPA/TW
60	tl	FLPA/ZE
66	t	JJ
68	tr	GI/TS/MT
70	tr	PA/PE/TC
	cl	FF/MH
	bl	LT/JL
71	tl	PA/PS
	c	FF/MH

	b	LB
72		PA/DR
76–77		HH/CM
77	tl	DD
78–79		GI/TS/PH
80	t	SS/JS
	b	LT/ML
83	br	GI/TS/MF
85	tl	MC/JC
	c	PA/DA
	bl	PM
	bc	FF/MH
86	b	HH/CM
91		GI/TS/PH
92	t	HH/NG
	b	HH/GW
93		MC/JC
94	tl	AB
	tr	HH/BB
97	t	GI/TS/TSt
	cr	MC/PM
	br	MC/JC
98	tl	MF
99	t	ABI
	c	MC/JC
100	br	MF
102–103		HH/CM
104	b	DrLM
106		MC/JC
107	l/r	MC/JC
112	l/r	DrLM
113		ABI
115	tr	HH/CM
	b	JM
116		MC/JC
117	bl	HH/CM
	br	MC/JC
118	t/b	CC
119	t/cr	FF/MH
120		DrLM

121	tl	GI/TS/AB
	cr	MF
124		SIL/MC
125	t	MC/JC
	c	HH/CR
126–127		MC/JC
128	t	MC/JC
131	t	MC/JC
132		MC/JC
134	tr	GI/TS/MT
	cl	MC/JC
	b	HH/WF
135	t	SS/DWi
136	tl	HH/PC
	c	HH/CM
138–139		PA/PE/P&LA
140	t	INC
	b	PB
141		I/RF
142–3	bl/br	NSRI
144	tr/bl	BHP
145		ABI
146	t	IT
	bl–br	GA
147		ABI
148	bl	GI/TS/RM
149		MF
150	t	LT/DS
	bl	PA/GdP
151	t	ER
	b	I/TI
152	tr	GE
	bl	PA/PE
153	t	GI/TS/MM
	b	HH/RB
154		GI/TS/JJa
155	tr	I/PIS
	b	FLPA/SMc